Vancouver

Travel Guide

A Complete Preparation and Vacation Guidebook to Exploring British Columbia's coastal Gem; Beaches, Rich History, culture and Hidden Gems

ADELINE M. CREEL

All Rights Reserved!

No part of this book may be reproduced, stored in a retrieval system, or transmitted in any form or by any means, electronic, mechanical, photocopying, recording, or otherwise, without the prior written permission of the copyright owner. Copyright 2024, Adeline M. Creel.

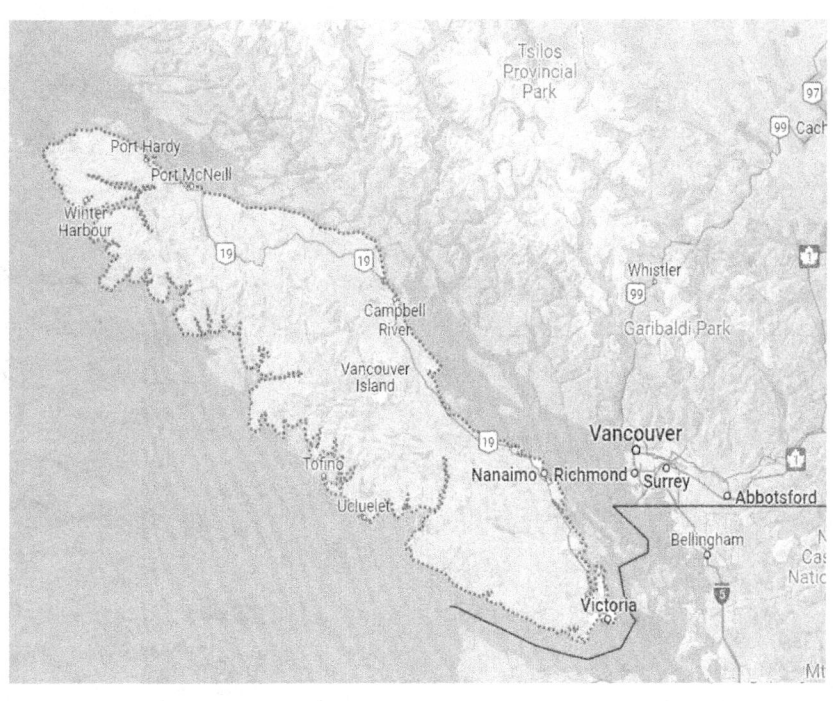

TABLE OF CONTENT

Introduction to Vancouver Island! 9
History of Vancouver Island. 14
    Geography and Climate 16
Planning for Your Trip to Vancouver Island 19
    Best time to visit 19
    Travel Essentials. 21
    Visa & Entry Requirements 22
    Local Laws and Customs 22
    Health and Safety Tips. 23
    Travel Advice for Families, Solo Travelers, and Couples 24
Transportation: Getting to and Around Vancouver Island 26
    Getting to Vancouver Island. 26
    Getting Around Vancouver Island. 28
    Public Transportation 29
    Specialty Transportation 30
Accommodations on Vancouver Island 32
    Budget Accommodations. 32
    Camping and RV Parks 33
    Budget Hotels 34
    Mid-range Accommodations 34
    Boutique hotels 35
    Luxury accommodations. 35
    Resorts 36
    Private villas and vacation rentals 36
Culinary Delights on Vancouver Island 38
    Seafood: Fresh From the Ocean 38
    Farm-to-table Dining 41

Craft breweries and distilleries 42
Bakeries and Cafes 46
Unique Culinary Experiences 47
Cooking School and Workshops 50
Street Food and Food Trucks 51
Victoria: The Cultural Heart of Vancouver Island 54
    Historic Foundations and Colonial Architecture 54
    Artistic Vitality and Cultural Institutions 56
    Culinary delights and local cuisine. 58
    Local Brews and Vineyards 59
    Community Festivals and Events 59
Nanaimo: The Harbour City of Vancouver Island 62
    Historical significance. 62
    Cultural Attractions 63
    Outdoor Activities 64
    The culinary scene 66
    Farm-to-table restaurants 67
Tofino: Surfing and Beaches 70
    The surfers' paradise 70
    Beyond the surf 72
    Wildlife and Scenic Views 73
    Outdoor Adventures and Activities 74
    Culinary delights and local cuisine. 75
    Cultural Experiences and Community Events 77
    Sustainable tourism and conservation efforts. 78
Comox Valley: Nature and Serenity. 80
    The Natural Beauty of Comox Valley. 80
    Cultural and Historical Richness 82
    Colonial History and Heritage Sites 83

Outdoor Adventures and Activities 84
Culinary delights and local cuisine. 86
Annual Events and Festivals 88
Wellness & Relaxation 89
Port Hardy: Gateway to the Wilderness. 92
Natural Wonders and Scenic Beauty 92
Cultural Heritage and Community Spirit 94
Outdoor adventure and recreational activities. 97
Outdoor Activities on Vancouver Island 104
Hiking: Exploring Vancouver Island on Foot. 104
Biking: Exploring the Island on Two Wheels. 107
Water Activities: Kayaking, Canoeing, and More. 110
Other Outdoor Adventures 113
Whale Watching and Wildlife Tours on Vancouver Island. 117
The Spectacle of Whale Watching 117
Best Places for Whale Watching 119
Wildlife Tours: Beyond the Whales 120
Plan Your Wildlife Adventure 122
Indigenous Cultural Experiences on Vancouver Island. 129
Understanding Indigenous Heritage 130
Immersive Cultural Tours 131
Cultural Centres and Museums 132
Traditional Art and Craft 133
Festivals and ceremonies 135
Cuisine and Traditional Foods 136
Learning & Educational Experiences 138
Museums and Historical Sites on Vancouver Island 142
Beaches and Coastal Wonders on Vancouver Island 155
Events & Festivals on Vancouver Island 166

Seasonal Festivals and Events.. 166
Practical Information for Travelers to Vancouver Island................... 179
    Safety & Security 179
    Health and Medical Services 182
    Connectivity and Communication 186
    Additional Practical Tips 188
    Language & Communication 189
Conclusion 192
    Tips for an unforgettable visit 192
Appendix 199
    Useful Apps 199
    Emergency Contacts 200
    FAQs 200
    Travel Checklist 202
    Travel Itineraries 203

Introduction to Vancouver Island!

Nestled off the southern coast of British Columbia, Vancouver Island has a stunning patchwork of forested mountains, enchanting rainforests, and wide beaches. This tour will take you on a journey to discover the island's diverse communities, rich culture, and breathtaking natural beauty.

Vancouver Island provides an escape into a world where nature and culture coexist. It is the largest island on North America's Pacific coast, measuring over 31,000 square kilometers. The island's diverse ecosystems span from the mist-shrouded temperate rainforests of the west coast to the rough, rocky coastlines of the east, with each having its distinct allure.

The island is more than simply a retreat for those seeking peace and adventure in its natural surroundings; it is also a cultural hotspot with profound Indigenous origins and a thriving contemporary art scene. The neighboring settlements, from the busy city of Victoria to the surf town of Tofino, are bright and hospitable, each giving its unique flavor to the island's overall appeal.

Starting in the south, Victoria, the provincial capital, combines historical charm with modern sophistication. The city's heritage architecture, bustling harbors, and dynamic public markets coexist with a variety of museums, galleries, and theatres. Beyond the metropolitan allure, the southern portion of the island is filled with serene suburbs, parks, and beaches, ideal for unhurried days spent exploring nature.

As you travel north, the central part of the island offers a contrast with its more rocky scenery and limited population. The region is great for people looking to detach and immerse themselves in nature. Central Vancouver Island is home to old woods, tranquil lakes, and some of the island's most difficult hiking paths.

The northern reaches of Vancouver Island are less traveled, yet they provide some of the most raw and pristine beauty. This location serves as a gateway to distant wilderness areas and is popular with outdoor enthusiasts who enjoy fishing, kayaking, and hiking.

Vancouver Island is also recognized for its wide variety of outdoor activities. The island's topography provides excellent options for hiking, mountain biking, and camping. The West Coast Trail, one of Canada's most well-known hiking trails, promises an exciting journey through lush forests and along gorgeous coastlines. Meanwhile, the waters around the island are ideal for whale watching, sailing, and kayaking, giving visitors close experiences with marine creatures in their natural habitat.

For those looking for a more tranquil pace, the island's various spas, yoga retreats, and wellness centers provide an ideal escape. The region's natural hot springs and calm, secluded locations make it a great getaway for anyone seeking to revitalize their bodies and minds.

The cultural heritage of Vancouver Island is profound and profoundly embedded in daily life. The island's First Nations groups, which include the Kwakwaka'wakw, Nuu-chah-nulth, and Coast Salish peoples, continue to celebrate their legacy, providing tourists with opportunities to learn about their rich traditions, art, and history. Cultural festivals, art exhibitions, and museums throughout the island offer glimpses into the rich indigenous cultures as well as the European colonial past that has shaped the region.

Vancouver Island is also a sanctuary for foodies. The moderate climate and good soil make it perfect for farming and agriculture. As a result, local markets are constantly stocked with fresh produce. Seafood is popular here, with local recipes featuring freshly caught salmon, halibut, and crab. The island's thriving wine sector and expanding number of craft brewers add another depth to its gastronomic scene, making it a must-see for both gourmets and connoisseurs.

Vancouver Island is a microcosm of nature's greatest qualities, interwoven with a rich tapestry of culture and history. Whether you desire adventure, relaxation, or cultural enrichment, the island has a wide range of activities and experiences that will make your vacation memorable. With this guide in hand, you'll be well-prepared to discover Vancouver Island's numerous wonders. Prepare to be fascinated by the island's breathtaking scenery, friendly locals, and limitless opportunities for adventure and exploration.

History of Vancouver Island.

Vancouver Island, a famous piece of territory tucked on Canada's western border, has a rich and varied history dating back thousands of years. From its first Indigenous occupants to European explorers and settlers, each age has left an indelible stamp on the island's cultural environment.

Long before European explorers set foot on Vancouver Island, it was home to a thriving and diversified community of Indigenous people. These groups, which included the Kwakwaka'wakw, Nuu-chah-nulth, and Coast Salish peoples, had a rich cultural heritage and strong relationships with the land. They created complex societies with social structures, economics, and spiritual beliefs that were inextricably linked to the natural world around them. Their control of the island's resources, from the cedar trees to the plentiful marine life, allowed them to thrive throughout millennia.

The Pacific Northwest's earliest European explorers arrived in the late 18th century. Captain James Cook was among the first to arrive on Vancouver Island, in 1778. This marked the beginning of greater European interest in the region, which was fueled first by the fur trade and then by territorial expansion ambitions. The Hudson's Bay organization, a major fur-trading organization, founded Fort Victoria in 1843, laying the groundwork for what would become Victoria, the island's main city and the capital of British Columbia.

The arrival of Europeans had far-reaching and often fatal repercussions on Indigenous populations, ranging from disease to displacement. Despite these problems, Vancouver Island's Indigenous peoples have kept and revitalized their cultures, and they continue to have a strong presence on the island.

Throughout the nineteenth and twentieth centuries, Vancouver Island expanded significantly. The discovery of gold on the British Columbia mainland in the 1850s fueled an influx of people and the expansion of Victoria as a major port and supply base. Logging and fishing grew to be key activities on the island, influencing both the economy and the landscape.

In recent years, Vancouver Island has gained recognition for its progressive environmental policies, strong technological sector, and expanding tourism industry, attracting visitors from all over the world drawn to its natural beauty and dynamic culture.

Geography and Climate

Vancouver Island, separated from the rest of British Columbia by the Strait of Georgia and the Queen Charlotte Strait, and from Washington State by the Juan de Fuca Strait, is a place of stark contrasts. Its rocky coastline, which stretches 3,400 kilometers, is a mosaic of bays, inlets, and fjords, while its interior is characterized by deep woods and mountains.

The island's geography is diverse, with the northern and center parts featuring dense, temperate rainforests, towering mountains, and secluded beaches. The southern section of the island, particularly around Victoria, has gentler terrain, with undulating hills and fewer mountain ranges. This region also supports the majority of the island's population and agricultural operations.

Climate zones

Vancouver Island is noted for having one of Canada's most temperate climates. It has a maritime climate, with moderate, rainy winters and cold, dry summers.

Coastal Regions: The island's west coast, particularly Tofino, is known for heavy rainfall, which helps to sustain the area's lush, dense forests. Fog is widespread throughout the summer, giving the area a mystical appearance.

Inland and Northern Areas: As you move inland and north, the weather becomes slightly cooler and more changeable. Snow covers mountain peaks virtually all year, and winters can be more severe than in coastal places.

Eastern and Southern Areas: The eastern and southern coastlines, which are protected from Pacific storms, have the driest temperatures on the island. These places, particularly the Victoria region, experience the mildest weather, with more sunny days and less precipitation than the rest of the island.

The history and geography of Vancouver Island are as diverse as the ecosystems and civilizations that inhabit it. Its history is one of persistence and adaptation, from ancient Indigenous civilizations to thriving modern metropolis. Geographically, it has everything from tranquil beaches to snow-capped mountains, with each region contributing to the island's distinct temperature and alluring charm. As you explore this book and the island itself, you'll come across a place where the past and present combine effortlessly, producing a dynamic and enriching experience for those who visit.

Planning for Your Trip to Vancouver Island

Visiting Vancouver Island offers a variety of experiences, from visiting calm forests and coastal beaches to connecting with lively metropolis cultures. To truly enjoy everything the island has to offer, proper planning is required. This section contains a detailed overview of the best time to visit, travel essentials, visa and entry procedures, local laws and customs, health and safety tips, and personalized information for families, lone travelers, and couples.

Best time to visit

The best time to visit Vancouver Island is determined by your plans for your stay. The island's climate is very mild by Canadian standards, making it a year-round attraction.

Spring (March to May): This season is ideal for individuals who appreciate the blooming of flowers and the mild weather. Victoria's famous Butchart

Gardens are in full bloom, displaying a beautiful array of vegetation.

Summer (June through August): is ideal for beachgoers and outdoor enthusiasts. The weather is the warmest of the year, ideal for hiking, kayaking, and animal watching. The Victoria International Jazz Fest and the Tofino Food and Wine Festival are just two of the many festivals and events that take place during the summer months.

Autumn (September to November): is an ideal season for individuals who enjoy calm exploration and spectacular autumn colors. Many whale species migrate along the coast during this season, making it a good time to see them.

Winter (December to February): Although cooler and rainier, winter on Vancouver Island is warmer than in much of Canada. This season is great for storm watching, which is a popular pastime in Tofino, as well as visiting indoor sites in Victoria, such as the Royal BC Museum.

Travel Essentials.

When packing for Vancouver Island, consider the activities you intend to participate in and the time of year you will be visiting:

Clothing: Layering is essential. Include waterproof materials and a durable pair of walking shoes. If you're traveling in the summer, wear light clothing but be prepared for chilly evenings.

Gear: Depending on your activities, you may require hiking footwear, camping gear, or surfing equipment. Many establishments offer rentals if you don't want to bring your own.

Travel Documents: Always bring your identification, travel insurance information, and any other necessary travel documents. If you intend to drive, be sure you have a driver's license and understand the rental conditions.

Visa & Entry Requirements

Travelers to Vancouver Island, as part of Canada, must comply with Canadian visa and entry regulations. Citizens of nations other than the United States will often require a visa or an Electronic Travel Authorization (eTA) to enter:

Visa: is required for several nationalities. Check the Government of Canada's official website for details, and apply well in advance of your trip.

eTA: Citizens of visa-exempt nations must get an eTA before flying into Canada. This is simply obtained online and electronically linked to your passport.

Local Laws and Customs

Understanding and following local laws and customs is critical.

Alcohol and Smoking: The legal drinking age is nineteen. Tobacco and cannabis use are restricted, with designated smoking places and limits near public buildings and parks.

Environment: Littering and environmental conservation laws are strictly enforced. Always stay on defined routes and obey wildlife warnings.

Health and Safety Tips.

Although Vancouver Island is typically safe, the following precautions should be taken:

Health Insurance: Make sure you have enough health insurance coverage. Medical care is great, but it might be costly for tourists without insurance.

Emergency Services: Familiarize yourself with local emergency numbers and nearby medical facilities.

Wildlife: Keep an eye out for wildlife while visiting natural regions. Store food securely and keep a safe distance from animals.

Travel Advice for Families, Solo Travelers, and Couples

Families should look for family-friendly lodgings and activities. Many sites and restaurants welcome children and frequently provide special activities to keep younger guests engaged.

Solo Travelers: Join community events and guided excursions to meet new people. Vancouver Island is noted for its nice people and safe environment.

Couples: Consider romantic holidays such as cozy beachside cabins or vineyard tours. The island's natural splendor is an ideal setting for a romantic getaway.

Preparing adequately for your visit to Vancouver Island can significantly improve your experience. You may ensure a smooth, enjoyable stay by planning ahead of time, packing carefully, understanding admission requirements, and being aware of local regulations and health recommendations. Whether you are a family searching for excitement, a solitary traveler looking for serenity, or a couple on a romantic holiday, Vancouver Island has a variety of experiences to make your journey special.

Transportation: Getting to and Around Vancouver Island.

Efficient transit is critical to any successful vacation experience, especially on Vancouver Island, where the variety of landscapes, from bustling towns to remote nature locations, can present distinct obstacles and opportunities. This comprehensive guide will teach you all you need to know about visiting Vancouver Island and navigating its diverse terrain once you arrive.

Getting to Vancouver Island.

Vancouver Island is well-connected and accessible from both the Canadian mainland and international destinations. Understanding the numerous options available will allow you to arrange a seamless and hassle-free trip.

By Air.

Victoria International Airport (YYJ): Located just north of Victoria, this is the principal entry point for those flying to Vancouver Island. It operates multiple daily flights from major Canadian cities and select US destinations. The airport has vehicle rental services, taxis, and public transit available to help you reach to your ultimate destination on the island.

Nanaimo Airport (YCD) and Comox Valley Airport (YQQ): are smaller airports that service domestic flights and provide convenient access to the island's central and northern regions. They are especially beneficial for travelers who want to explore more isolated locations quickly.

By Sea

BC Ferries: This is one of the most scenic ways to go to Vancouver Island, with service from the mainland to Victoria, Nanaimo, and Sidney. The boats may transport passengers with or without automobiles, making them an adaptable alternative for a variety of travelers.

Private Boats and Yachts: For those seeking a more personalized travel experience or visiting from adjacent coastal communities, some various marinas and harbors accommodate private watercraft.

By Land.

Bus Services: Greyhound Canada and IslandLink offer bus services from mainland British Columbia to Vancouver Island that include a ferry ride. This option is suitable for individuals who do not wish to drive themselves.

Getting Around Vancouver Island.

Once on the island, the diversity of terrain, from urban centers to quiet beaches and hilly areas, necessitates a strategic approach to mobility. Here's how to efficiently navigate the island:

By Car.

Renting a car is undoubtedly the most convenient method to discover Vancouver Island at your leisure. It gives you the freedom to visit rural spots and spectacular drives like the Pacific Marine Circle

Route. Car rentals are accessible at major airports and cities throughout the island.

Public Transportation

Buses: Public transport systems are available in major cities such as Victoria and Nanaimo, with services extended to smaller communities. BC Transit provides comprehensive bus services that are both economical and dependable for navigating urban regions.

Taxis and Rideshares: Taxis are widely available, particularly in major cities, while ridesharing services such as Uber have begun to establish themselves on the island, providing handy alternatives to traditional taxis.

By bicycle.

Vancouver Island is a cyclist's paradise, with several bike lanes and trails. Cities such as Victoria have extensive cycling paths, making bicycles an attractive option for both recreation and transportation. Bike rentals are offered in most major tourist destinations.

Walking

Walking is not only a relaxing method to explore Vancouver Island's breathtaking surroundings, but it is also useful in smaller towns and crowded urban areas such as downtown Victoria. Many of the island's attractions are near together, particularly in tourist regions.

Specialty Transportation

Water Taxis: In coastal places, water taxis can transport you to islands and remote coastal communities that are not accessible by road. This is very popular in areas like Tofino and Ucluelet.

Scenic Flights: To get a new perspective, arrange a scenic flight above the island. Several firms provide helicopter or light plane tours with amazing aerial views of the island's terrain.

Whether you arrive by air, sea, or land, and whether you choose to explore by car, bus, bike, or foot, Vancouver Island's transport options are as varied as the island itself. Each mode of transportation has its own set of benefits, allowing you to personalize your travel experience to your specific interests, itinerary, and the type of sites you want to see. With proper planning, getting to and around Vancouver Island may be an important aspect of your vacation, enriching your travel experience.

Accommodations on Vancouver Island

When planning a trip to Vancouver Island, choosing the correct accommodations is critical to your whole experience. The island has a wide variety of hotel alternatives to suit all preferences and budgets, ranging from cozy, low-cost hostels to magnificent beachfront resorts. This extensive guide analyses the range of lodgings available, ensuring that you locate the ideal location to stay, whether you're looking for a low-cost choice or a luxurious escape.

Budget Accommodations.

For visitors wishing to extend their vacation without breaking the bank, Vancouver Island has a variety of economical accommodations.

Hostels and Backpacker Lodges

Ocean Island Inn | Backpackers | Suites: Located in the center of Victoria, this dynamic hostel has both dormitory beds and private rooms, making it ideal for lone travelers or budget-conscious groups. There is a kitchen, free WiFi, and organized social events.

HI Tofino, Whaler's on the Point Guesthouse: Located in Tofino, this hostel offers breathtaking views of Clayoquot Sound and convenient access to surfing beaches and hiking trails. It's an excellent choice for nature enthusiasts seeking a low-cost stay.

Camping and RV Parks

Living Forest Oceanside Campground & RV Park: Located in Nanaimo, this campground spans over 50 acres of forest and seashore, providing amenities for tents and RVs. It's an excellent alternative for families and travelers seeking to reconnect with nature.

Goldstream Provincial Park Campground: located near Victoria, provides a low-cost camping experience with stunning landscapes and opportunities to watch local species such as bald eagles and river salmon.

Budget Hotels

Red Lion Inn and Suites: Located in downtown Victoria, this hotel provides comfortable, reasonable lodgings with amenities such as a swimming pool and on-site restaurant, making it an excellent choice for budget-conscious travelers.

Travelodge by Wyndham Parksville: This hotel offers affordable accommodation with beach access and is conveniently located near local activities, making it ideal for families and budget travelers.

Mid-range Accommodations

For those looking for a comfortable stay without the luxury price tag, mid-range hotels and bed and breakfasts provide the ideal blend of comfort and affordability.

Bed & Breakfasts

The Gingerbread Cottage Bed & Breakfast: in Victoria provides a warm, inviting ambiance with handmade breakfasts and personalized service.

Two Eagles Lodge: Located in Courtenay, this bed and breakfast overlooks the Strait of Georgia and offers spacious rooms with modern conveniences, making it ideal for a relaxing vacation.

Boutique hotels

The Oswego Hotel: is a boutique hotel in Victoria recognized for its contemporary style and personalized service. It's a short walk from the waterfront and has fully furnished kitchens in each accommodation.

Tofino Harbourview Motel: is a cozy, family-run motel with easy access to Tofino's magnificent beaches and local eateries, ideal for people wishing to experience the area's natural beauty.

Luxury accommodations.

Luxury lodgings on Vancouver Island offer stunning settings and first-rate services for the ultimate relaxation and indulgence.

Resorts

The Wickaninnish Inn: located on Tofino's rocky west coast, is a world-renowned luxury resort that provides spectacular ocean views, a full-service spa, and great cuisine. It represents the pinnacle of rustic elegance and Pacific Northwest grandeur.

Fairmont Empress: This historic Victoria hotel, which overlooks the Inner Harbour, has represented elegance and sophistication since 1908. With its timeless appeal, award-winning spa, and afternoon tea service, it remains a popular choice for visitors wanting a regal experience.

Private villas and vacation rentals

Pacific Sands Beach Resort Villas: Offering private beachfront villas in Tofino, these accommodations are ideal for families and couples seeking a home away from home with breathtaking views and easy beach access.

Bear Mountain Resort: Mountainside Luxury Residences - Located in Langford, these opulent residences have golf course views, high-end amenities, and spacious accommodations, making them ideal for extended upmarket stays.

Vancouver Island's lodging options cater to all types of visitors. Whether you're trekking on a shoestring budget, taking a comfortable mid-range holiday, or treating yourself to a luxury break, the island has something for everyone. Each form of lodging not only gives a place to stay but also improves your overall experience on the island, whether through direct proximity to nature, exposure to local culture, or pampering amenities that make your trip unique.

Culinary Delights on Vancouver Island

Vancouver Island is a culinary paradise, with a diversified cultural heritage and ample natural resources. The island's food culture is robust and diverse, with fresh seafood and locally sourced produce alongside world-class vineyards and inventive eateries. This book looks into the culinary delights of Vancouver Island, showcasing the greatest locations to dine, drink, and enjoy the island's distinct flavors.

Seafood: Fresh From the Ocean

Given its coastal position, it's hardly surprising that seafood is a staple of Vancouver Island's culinary scene. The surrounding waterways are teeming with fish, shellfish, and other marine pleasures, providing a plethora of fresh ingredients to local cooks.

Salmon

Salmon is possibly the best-recognised seafood on Vancouver Island. It is a popular ingredient on many menus, whether it is caught wild or grown responsibly.

Salmon Houses: Restaurants such as The Salmon House in Tofino and Sooke Harbour House are well-known for their masterfully prepared salmon meals. Whether smoked, grilled, or baked, the salmon is always fresh and tasty.

Salmon Festivals: The island organizes several salmon-themed events, including the Port Alberni Salmon Festival, which offers tourists a variety of salmon meals, cooking demos, and fishing competitions.

Shellfish

Shellfish, including oysters, clams, mussels, and crabs, abound in the clean seas around Vancouver Island.

Fanny Bay Oysters: is a leading supplier of oysters and other seafood. Their oysters, famed for their sweet and briny flavor, can be savored at a variety of local eateries or purchased straight from the farm.

Crab Feasts: Many coastal villages, including Ucluelet and Comox, host yearly crab festivals where freshly caught Dungeness crabs are the main attraction. These gatherings frequently feature crab boils, cooking competitions, and several opportunities to sample this local delicacy.

Halibut with Other Fish

Halibut, cod, rockfish, and other indigenous species are staples of the island's seafood menu.

Fish & Chips: No vacation to Vancouver Island is complete without trying the island's famous fish and chips. Go-to restaurants include Red Fish Blue Fish in Victoria, which serves sustainable fish in a relaxed waterfront setting, and The Codfather in Nanaimo, which is famous for its crispy, golden-battered halibut.

Farm-to-table Dining

The abundant soil and warm climate of Vancouver Island support a vibrant agricultural business, leading to a strong farm-to-table movement. Local chefs take delight in using fresh, seasonal ingredients from surrounding farms and markets.

Farmers' Markets

Farmers' markets on the island are packed with fresh vegetables, handmade goods, and gastronomic pleasures.

Moss Street Market: located in Victoria, serves as a nexus for local farmers, bakers, and crafters. Visitors can peruse stalls stocked with organic veggies, fresh berries, handcrafted jams, and gourmet cheese.

Comox Valley Farmers' Market: This market is popular among both locals and visitors. It offers a wide range of fresh fruit, meats, dairy products, and baked items, all made by local farmers and craftsmen.

Farm-to-table restaurants

Restaurants on Vancouver Island have embraced the farm-to-table mentality, using the best local ingredients on their menu.

Acres Bistro: In Victoria, 10 Acres Bistro gets much of its produce from its organic farm. The menu changes seasonally, with meals highlighting the freshest ingredients available.

Ravenstone Farm Artisan Meat Shop: Located near Qualicum Beach, this farm-to-table restaurant specializes in pasture-raised meat. Their farm store sells a range of chops, sausages, and charcuterie created from animals farmed on the farm.

Craft breweries and distilleries

Vancouver Island has a thriving craft beer and spirits culture, with many breweries and distilleries producing creative and award-winning products.

Craft breweries

The island is home to a burgeoning craft beer culture, with brewers ranging from small, family-run businesses to larger, more established brands.

Driftwood Brewery: Located in Victoria, Driftwood Brewery is noted for its robust and distinctive beers. Their Fat Tug IPA is popular among hop enthusiasts, and their seasonal releases highlight the brewers' ingenuity.

Tofino Brewing Company: Located in the surfing hamlet of Tofino, this brewery serves a variety of beers that represent the laid-back atmosphere of the area. Their Tuff Session Ale and Kelp Stout are very popular.

Distilleries

The island's distilleries manufacture a wide range of spirits, including gin, vodka, whisky, and liqueurs.

Sheringham Distillery: This award-winning distillery near Sooke is well-known for its botanical gin and seashore gin, both of which use locally sourced ingredients. Their spirits have received international recognition, making them a must-try for every spirits fan.

Wayward Distillery: Located in Courtenay, Wayward Distillery makes a variety of spirits, including honey-based vodka and gin. Their unorthodox approach and dedication to quality have set them apart in the local distilling scene.

Wineries and Vineyards

Vancouver Island's wine sector has grown in recent years, with vineyards producing high-quality wines that represent the region's distinct terroir.

Wine Regions

The Cowichan Valley, Saanich Peninsula, and Comox Valley are the island's three primary wine areas.

Cowichan Valley: Known as the island's wine district, the Cowichan Valley is home to several wineries, including Averill Creek Vineyard and Blue Grouse Estate Winery. The region's warm atmosphere is perfect for grape cultivation, producing wines with rich, nuanced flavors.

The Saanich Peninsula: located just north of Victoria, has several notable vineyards, including Church & State Wines and De Vine Vineyards. Visitors can enjoy tastings and excursions while admiring the breathtaking views of the surrounding countryside.

Wine festivals and events.

Throughout the year, Vancouver Island holds several wine festivals and events to celebrate the region's expanding wine industry.

Cowichan Valley Wine Festival: Held every August, this festival includes wine tastings, vineyard tours, and special events at participating wineries. It's an excellent opportunity to discover the region and taste some of its finest wines.

Vancouver Island Wine Awards: This yearly competition recognizes the best wines made on the island. The awards ceremony, which is frequently accompanied by a gala event, celebrates the best of Vancouver Island's winemaking skills.

Bakeries and Cafes

The island's bakeries and cafés serve a delicious selection of freshly baked delicacies, artisanal breads, and gourmet coffee.

Artisan bakeries

From traditional breads to inventive pastries, Vancouver Island's bakeries are known for producing high-quality, handcrafted items.

Fol Epi: Located in Victoria, Fol Epi is well-known for its organic, wood-fired breads and exquisite pastry. The bakery's dedication to using local and organic ingredients is evident in every taste.

True Grain: with outlets in Cowichan Bay and Mill Bay, specializes in classic European-style bread and pastries. Their emphasis on whole grains and natural fermentation methods yields superior flavor and texture.

Cozy cafes

The island's cafés offer a comfortable environment for having a cup of coffee or a light meal.

Habit Coffee: A Victoria staple, Habit Coffee is noted for its expertly made espresso drinks and cozy, modern atmosphere. The café sources its beans from ethical and sustainable farmers to provide a high-quality coffee experience.

The Wandering Moose Café: Located in Cumberland, this lovely café serves coffee, tea, and fresh baked products. Its peaceful, rustic atmosphere makes it an ideal place to unwind after a day of touring.

Unique Culinary Experiences

For those looking for something a little different, Vancouver Island has several unique culinary experiences that highlight the island's inventive spirit and dedication to excellence.

Farm Dinner and Culinary Tours

Several farms and organizations on the island provide farm-to-table meals and culinary excursions, giving guests an immersive experience that highlights the best of local cuisine and wine.

Feast Tofino: This yearly festival in Tofino includes a series of collaborative dinners, cooking seminars, and special events that highlight the region's culinary expertise and local resources. It's a must-attend for foodies eager to sample the best of Tofino's culinary scene.

North Island College Culinary Programs: North Island College provides culinary programs in Campbell River and Courtenay, including public dinners and events. These events allow students to demonstrate their abilities while also presenting guests with an unforgettable eating experience.

Indigenous cuisine.

Indigenous culinary traditions play an important role in Vancouver Island's food culture. Many Indigenous-owned companies and organizations provide an opportunity to learn about these rich and diverse culinary traditions.

Kekuli Café: with sites in Duncan and beyond, serves a menu influenced by traditional Indigenous cuisine. The café is well-known for its bannock, a sort of frybread that is popular in many Indigenous communities and comes with a variety of toppings and fillings.

Salmon n' Bannock Bistro, located in Victoria, delivers contemporary meals with traditional Indigenous flavors. The menu includes locally derived delicacies such as wild game, seafood, and berries, cooked using both modern and traditional methods.

Cooking School and Workshops

For individuals wishing to improve their culinary skills, Vancouver Island has several cooking schools and workshops.

The London Chef

The London Chef, based in Victoria, provides hands-on cooking instruction in a variety of cuisines and methods. Professional chefs provide classes that emphasize the use of fresh, locally sourced ingredients.

North Island College's Culinary Arts

North Island College's Campbell River and Courtenay campuses both offer extensive culinary arts programs. In addition to formal instruction, the institution provides community culinary classes and workshops, where participants can learn new skills and methods.

Cooking with Company

This unique culinary experience provides private cooking instruction in the comfort of your own home. Professional chefs lead participants through the preparation of a gourmet meal, sharing insights and methods along the way.

Street Food and Food Trucks

The street food scene on Vancouver Island is dynamic and diversified, with a wide variety of flavors and cuisines.

Tacofino

Tacofino, which began as a food truck in Tofino, has since become a treasured island staple. Tacofino, known for its fresh and tasty tacos, burritos, and other Mexican-inspired cuisine, has expanded to include trucks in Victoria and Tofino.

The authentic poutine and burgers.

This food truck provides a taste of Quebec with its authentic poutine and gourmet burgers.

L'Authentique, located in Victoria, is a popular destination for both locals and visitors.

Pig's BBQ Joint

Pig BBQ Joint specializes in southern-style barbecue, serving great smoked meats, sandwiches, and sides. Their food truck may be located in several locations throughout Victoria, serving delicious meals on the go.

The culinary scene on Vancouver Island is as diverse and dynamic as the landscapes themselves. From fresh seafood and farm-to-table dining to craft beverages and one-of-a-kind food experiences, the island provides a diverse range of flavors that reflect its cultural legacy and natural wealth.

Whether you're a die-hard foodie or just searching for a delicious meal, Vancouver Island promises a culinary excursion that will delight your senses and leave you with unforgettable memories. As you explore the island's culinary delights, you'll find the creativity, passion, and dedication that distinguish Vancouver Island as a true culinary destination.

Victoria: The Cultural Heart of Vancouver Island

Victoria, British Columbia's capital city, is the bustling cultural hub of Vancouver Island. Victoria, known for its historic buildings, bustling harbors, and beautiful gardens, is a city where the past and present combine perfectly, creating a rich tapestry of experiences that attracts visitors from all over the world. This extensive exploration delves into Victoria's essence, stresses its important cultural characteristics such as historical landmarks, artistic venues, gastronomic experiences, and community events.

Historic Foundations and Colonial Architecture

Victoria's history is steeped in both Indigenous cultures and European colonial influences, making it a distinct cultural powerhouse on Vancouver Island.

The city's architecture tells a visual story about its past.

The British influence

The Parliament Buildings: Designed by architect Francis Rattenbury in the late nineteenth century, these majestic structures serve as a reminder of Victoria's colonial history and are a prominent point along the Inner Harbour. Free guided tours provide insight into British Columbia's political past as well as the buildings' architectural elegance.

Craigdarroch Castle: The home, erected by coal baron Robert Dunsmuir in the late 1800s, represents the opulent lifestyles of the era's wealthy. The castle's elaborate Victorian architecture and meticulously renovated rooms offer a glimpse into the splendor of the past, and it now serves as a museum, attracting history buffs from all around.

Indigenous Heritage

Royal BC Museum: This well-known museum presents both natural and human history, with a focus on Indigenous artifacts and cultural exhibits. The First Peoples' Gallery, in particular, provides a detailed look at the lives of the native communities that have inhabited British Columbia for thousands of years. Artifacts, artwork, and multimedia presentations bring these cultures' rich tapestry to life, giving visitors a thorough grasp of the region's history.

Artistic Vitality and Cultural Institutions

Victoria is more than simply a historical building; it is also a vibrant center for arts and culture. The city has a thriving arts culture, with various galleries, theatres, and live music venues catering to all tastes.

The Art Community

The Art Gallery of Greater Victoria boasts an exceptional collection of both historical and contemporary art, with a focus on works by

Canadian and Pacific Northwest artists, as well as a major collection of Asian artwork. The gallery's displays are carefully organized to represent both local and international perspectives.

Belfry Theatre: Located in the historic Fernwood neighborhood, this professional not-for-profit theatre presents a diverse range of plays throughout the year, including current Canadian works and recreated classics, all performed by great local and national actors.

Music & Performance

Victoria Symphony Orchestra: The Victoria Symphony Orchestra, one of Canada's most famous orchestras, delivers a diverse repertoire of classical and contemporary works in the magnificent Royal Theatre. Locals and visitors alike enjoy their seasonal concerts, which include the famed Symphony Splash, an outdoor concert on the Inner Harbour.

Victoria Jazz Group: Through its annual JazzFest and monthly concerts, this group has been a driving force in bringing international jazz performers to the city, improving Victoria's musical landscape, and offering a platform for a diverse range of jazz styles from around the world.

Culinary delights and local cuisine.

Victoria's food scene reflects its rich culture. Because of the city's location on the Pacific coast, fresh seafood is a must-have, while a thriving agricultural hinterland provides a plethora of local vegetables for chefs to create both classic and inventive meals.

Dining Experiences

Inner Harbour Restaurants: Here, dining options range from fancy seafood restaurants to casual cafes, with many giving stunning views of the harbor. The emphasis is on fresh, locally produced foods, with dishes highlighting the finest of the region's offerings.

Chinatown: As Canada's oldest Chinatown, this dynamic neighborhood provides a variety of unique culinary experiences that represent the city's historical Chinese heritage. Visitors can eat anything from dim sum to hand-pulled noodles.

Local Brews and Vineyards

Victoria's Craft Beer Scene: Home to over a dozen craft brewers, Victoria is renowned as Canada's craft beer capital. Each brewery has its distinct style, ranging from classic ales to experimental beers with local elements such as spruce or seaweed.

The Saanich Peninsula Vineyards: located just a short drive from the city center, provide tastings and excursions. The chilly marine climate is ideal for creating crisp whites and exquisite red wines that are receiving international praise.

Community Festivals and Events

Victoria's communal spirit is evident in its festivals and celebrations, which honor everything from local culture and history to food and music.

Annual Highlights:

Victoria Day procession: One of the city's largest events, this procession commemorates Queen Victoria's birthday and features marching bands, cultural floats, and military displays, drawing spectators from all over the island and beyond.

Fringe Festival: As part of the international Fringe Festival movement, this event brings together a diverse range of performers in venues across the city, displaying everything from avant-garde theatre to comedy and dance.

Seasonal Activities.

Butchart Gardens Seasonal Displays: The famed gardens change with the seasons, from spring tulips to autumn chrysanthemums and stunning winter illuminations, giving visitors a new reason to come and enjoy the floral beauty.

Victoria, as the cultural hub of Vancouver Island, provides a rich, diverse tapestry of activities for fans of history, art, culinary delights, and community spirit. Victoria offers guests an unforgettable cultural adventure, whether they explore its historic buildings, attend a theatre, eat local food, or celebrate during a festival. This dynamic city continues to honor its history while embracing the progressive attitude that has made it a must-see destination on Canada's Pacific coast.

Nanaimo: The Harbour City of Vancouver Island

Nanaimo, sometimes known as the Harbour City, is a bustling town on Vancouver Island's eastern shores. Nanaimo is known for its bustling waterfront, rich history, and mix of urban and nature attractions, providing visitors with a one-of-a-kind experience. This exhaustive guide delves into the city's historical significance, cultural attractions, outdoor activities, culinary scene, and annual events, providing a thorough picture of what makes Nanaimo a must-see destination on Vancouver Island.

Historical significance.

Indigenous Heritage: Nanaimo, named after the Snuneymuxw First Nation, has thousands of years of history. The Snuneymuxw people have resided in the area since time immemorial, building a strong connection to the land and sea. Their rich cultural legacy may be discovered in a variety of locations throughout the city, including petroglyph parks and cultural centers that provide insight into their traditional way of life.

Coal Mining Era: The city's contemporary history began in the mid-nineteenth century, with the discovery of coal. Scottish entrepreneur Robert Dunsmuir was instrumental in growing Nanaimo's coal mining sector, which attracted workers and their families, transforming the city into a thriving hub. The Nanaimo Museum offers a detailed look at this era, including displays on coal mining and its impact on the city's history.

Cultural Attractions

Nanaimo Museum: The Nanaimo Museum, located in the center of downtown, takes visitors on a fascinating tour through the city's history. The museum's exhibits span a wide range of local history, including Indigenous artifacts, the coal mining era, and the notorious "Nanaimo Bar," a Canadian dessert invented in the city.

The Bastion: The Hudson's Bay Company built The Bastion, one of Nanaimo's most famous monuments, in 1853. This medieval wooden fortification acted as both a defense structure and a commercial post. Today, it serves as a museum, giving tourists a look into the early days of European settlement on the island.

The Port Theatre: The Port Theatre, a staple of Nanaimo's cultural landscape, produces a diverse range of acts, including theatre productions, concerts, and dance shows. With its cutting-edge facilities and diversified programming, the theatre is a cultural hub in the town, attracting both local and international talent.

Outdoor Activities

Nanaimo's natural beauty and outdoor possibilities are among its main attractions. From seaside parks to mountain paths, the city provides a wealth of activities for environment lovers.

Harbourfront Walkway: This panoramic path runs along Nanaimo's lovely waterfront, providing breathtaking views of the harbor, marinas, and coastal mountains. It's ideal for a relaxing stroll, jog, or bike ride. Along the journey, you'll see public artworks, cafes, and benches where you can unwind and take in the scenery.

Newcastle Island Marine Provincial Park: Newcastle Island, just a short ferry journey from downtown, provides an opportunity to reconnect with nature. The island has hiking and bike paths, sandy beaches, and historical attractions, including artifacts from the coal mining past. Picnics, camping, and animal watching are all popular activities here.

Mount Benson Regional Park: For those seeking adventure, Mount Benson has demanding climbing trails that reward climbers with panoramic views of Nanaimo and the surrounding area. On clear days, the peak offers a stunning vantage point with views of the Georgia Strait and the mainland.

Diving and Snorkeling: Nanaimo is famous for its outstanding diving and snorkeling opportunities. The area's seas are home to a broad range of marine life, including an artificial reef built by the purposefully sunk HMCS Saskatchewan, a former navy destroyer. Divers can visit this and other underwater sites year-round.

The culinary scene

Nanaimo's food culture is just as diversified as its population. The city provides a variety of dining experiences, from simple cafes to fine dining venues, many of which use locally sourced ingredients.

Seafood Delights: Given its seaside location, Nanaimo has some of the freshest seafood on Vancouver Island. Restaurants near the shoreline, including the famed Lighthouse Bistro & Pub, serve a variety of dishes incorporating locally caught fish, shrimp, and other seafood.

Nanaimo Bar Trail: No visit to Nanaimo is complete without indulging in the city's most famous dessert, the Nanaimo bar. This layered delight can be found at a variety of bakeries and cafes across the city. The Nanaimo Bar Trail offers a self-guided tour of some of the best places to sample this delectable treat in its conventional form or with creative tweaks.

Farm-to-table restaurants

Nanaimo's proximity to fertile farmland offers a consistent supply of fresh produce. Gabriel's Gourmet Cafe, for example, focuses on farm-to-table eating with seasonal menus that highlight the best local foods.

Annual Events and Festivals.

Nanaimo has a wide range of events and festivals throughout the year, honoring everything from arts and culture to food and sports.

Bathtub Race Festival: The annual Bathtub Racing Festival is one of Nanaimo's most unique events. Every summer, participants race motorized bathtubs across the harbor. The festival has a parade, fireworks, and a variety of family-friendly activities, making it a summertime highlight.

Nanaimo Marine Festival: The Nanaimo Marine Festival, which coincides with the Bathtub Racing Festival, commemorates the city's maritime heritage. The festival features live music, food sellers, and nautical-themed activities, attracting both visitors and locals to the waterfront.

Dragonboat Festival: The Nanaimo Dragon Boat Festival, which takes place yearly in Maffeo Sutton Park, is a colorful and lively event. Teams from all across the region compete in dragon boat races, and the event also includes cultural performances, food vendors, and a lively environment.

Summer Blues Festival: Music fans will enjoy the Summertime Blues Festival, which brings together local and worldwide blues musicians for a weekend of performances. The festival is held at the lovely Maffeo Sutton Park, which provides a scenic backdrop for live music.

Nanaimo, with its rich history, cultural attractions, outdoor activities, and dynamic culinary scene, certainly lives up to its nickname, the Harbour City. Nanaimo provides a unique and interesting experience for all tourists, whether they are visiting historical monuments, admiring natural beauty, trying local cuisine, or taking part in one of the city's numerous events. Its unique blend of urban charm and natural splendor distinguishes it as a standout destination on Vancouver Island, enticing visitors to explore and appreciate everything it has to offer.

Tofino: Surfing and Beaches

Tofino, located on the mountainous west coast of Vancouver Island, is a little community with some of Canada's most spectacular coastal landscapes. Tofino, known as Canada's surfing capital, is not only a haven for surfers, but also a utopia for nature lovers, beachgoers, and those looking for a peaceful retreat from the hustle and bustle of life. This book goes deeply into Tofino's attractiveness, examining its world-renowned beaches, surfing culture, and a plethora of outdoor activities that make this location a must-see.

The surfers' paradise

The Surf Culture: Tofino's reputation as a premier surfing location is well-earned. The village's relaxed environment, along with its breathtaking natural beauty, attracts surfers from all over the world.

Surfing History: Surfing became popular in Tofino in the 1960s, when the first surfers braved the frigid Pacific seas with basic equipment. Over the years, the sport has flourished, thanks to a lively community and the construction of surf schools and businesses.

Surf stores and Schools: Tofino has several surf stores and schools that provide rentals, lessons, and surf gear. Pacific Surf Co. and Surf Sister Surf School are well-known for catering to surfers of all skill levels, from novices eager to catch their first wave to experienced surfers seeking advanced coaching.

Top Surf Spots

Long Beach, arguably Tofino's most famous surfing area, is part of the Pacific Rim National Park Reserve. Its wide sandy beach and regular waves make it excellent for surfers of all abilities. The beach's natural beauty, which includes vistas of rolling waves against a backdrop of forested mountains, adds to its appeal.

Chesterman Beach: Divided into North and South Chesterman, this beach is ideal for surfing and discovering tide pools. South Chesterman is especially popular among novices due to its milder waves, whilst North Chesterman attracts more experienced surfers.

Cox Bay: is a popular destination for expert surfers due to its big waves. The beach also hosts various surf contests throughout the year, including the annual Rip Curl Pro Tofino, Canada's largest surfing competition.

Beyond the surf

While Tofino is renowned for surfing, its beaches have much more to offer than just excellent waves. The location offers numerous options for relaxation, adventure, and animal observation.

Beachcombing and Tidepools

Mackenzie Beach: A quieter alternative to the more renowned surfing beaches, Mackenzie Beach is ideal for families and individuals wishing to unwind. Its protected waters are great for swimming, kayaking, and paddleboarding. The beach is also ideal for beachcombing and visiting tide pools full of marine life.

Florencia Bay: Part of the Pacific Rim National Park Reserve, Florencia Bay provides a more private beach experience. It's a great place to wander, picnic, and watch the waves crash on the coast. The beach's secluded location provides a peaceful respite for anyone seeking to reconnect with nature.

Wildlife and Scenic Views

Wildlife Viewing: Tofino's coastal waters are home to a wide variety of marine life. Visitors frequently see grey whales, orcas, sea otters, and harbor seals. Several local operators provide whale-watching cruises, which allow you to get up close and personal with these majestic creatures.

Scenic Hiking paths: The Tofino area has various hiking paths that highlight the region's natural beauty. The Tonquin Trail is a short walk with breathtaking views of Clayoquot Sound and access to quiet beaches. For a more difficult walk, the Wild Pacific Trail in nearby Ucluelet offers magnificent coastal views and the opportunity to see eagles and other animals.

Outdoor Adventures and Activities

Aside from surfing, Tofino's natural setting is ideal for a range of outdoor sports.

Kayaking and canoeing: Exploring the seas of Tofino by kayak or canoe is a favorite pastime. The quiet waters of Clayoquot Sound allow paddlers to explore secret coves, isolated beaches, and thick forests. Guided excursions are available, providing information about the area's nature and Indigenous culture.

Fishing and Boat Tours: Tofino is an excellent destination for fishing aficionados. The seas surrounding the settlement are abundant with salmon, halibut, and other fish species. Charter services provide guided fishing expeditions for both novice and experienced anglers.

Hot Springs Cove: When in Tofino, you must visit Hot Springs Cove. Maquinna Marine Provincial Park is home to natural hot springs that can only be reached by boat or seaplane. The drive to the cove is an adventure in itself, with opportunities to see whales and other marine creatures.

Culinary delights and local cuisine.

Tofino's culinary culture reflects both the seaside setting and the active community. From fresh seafood to locally sourced delicacies, the village's restaurants provide a wide choice of dining options.

Fresh seafood.

Wolf in the Fog: This award-winning restaurant is a staple of Tofino's culinary scene. Wolf in the Fog is known for its inventive recipes and concentration on locally sourced ingredients, and its menu celebrates the Pacific Northwest's richness. Fresh shellfish, foraged veggies, and house-made charcuterie are standouts.

The Pointe Restaurant: located in the Wickaninnish Inn, provides beautiful ocean views and a wonderful dining experience. The menu highlights locally produced fish and products, with visually appealing and delectable dishes.

Casual Dining and Local Favorites.

Tacofino: What began as a food truck has grown into a local legend. Tacofino delivers some of the greatest tacos on the island, ranging from basic fish tacos to unique vegetarian versions.

Tofitian Café: A favorite among both locals and visitors, Tofitian serves delicious coffee, pastries, and small meals. It's the ideal place to begin your day before venturing out to explore the beaches and trails.

Cultural Experiences and Community Events

Tofino's robust community spirit shines through in its cultural events and festivals. Throughout the year, the town hosts several events to showcase its distinct culture and natural surroundings.

Tofino Film Festival: The Tofino Film Festival features a mix of local and international films, demonstrating the community's dedication to arts and culture. The festival offers screenings, workshops, and Q&A sessions with filmmakers.

Tofino Lantern Festival: The annual Tofino Lantern Festival is a magical event that draws the town together. Participants make homemade lanterns and parade through the village, brightening the night with a vibrant spectacle. The festival also includes live music, shows, and food vendors.

Pacific Rim Whale Festival: The Pacific Rim Whale Festival is a week-long festival that commemorates the yearly migration of grey whales. It includes educational programs, art exhibitions, and family activities. It is an excellent opportunity to learn about marine life and the value of conservation.

Sustainable tourism and conservation efforts.

Tofino is dedicated to conserving the natural environment and encouraging sustainable tourism. Many local companies and organizations promote conservation and environmental responsibility.

Tofino Botanical Gardens: The Tofino Botanical Gardens allow visitors to discover the rich flora of the Pacific Northwest. The gardens are also a center for education and conservation, with programs promoting sustainability and environmental awareness.

Clayoquot Biosphere Trust: This organization promotes conservation and sustainable development in the Clayoquot Sound UNESCO Biosphere Region. The Trust supports a wide range of community programs, including environmental education, research, and habitat restoration.

Tofino, with its beautiful beaches, world-class surfing, and diverse natural surroundings, provides a one-of-a-kind and spectacular travel experience. Tofino has something for everyone, whether you're an experienced surfer, a nature lover, or just want to relax and enjoy the beauty of the Pacific coast.

Its combination of outdoor experiences, gastronomic delights, cultural events, and dedication to sustainability make it a must-see destination on Vancouver Island. As you explore Tofino, you'll discover a community that values its natural environment and warmly welcomes visitors, asking you to join in the wonder of this coastal paradise.

Comox Valley: Nature and Serenity.

Nestled between the towering peaks of the Beaufort Mountain Range and the calm shores of the Salish Sea, Vancouver Island's Comox Valley is a retreat for visitors seeking nature and tranquility. This region, which includes the towns of Comox, Courtenay, and Cumberland, provides a diverse range of outdoor activities, scenic vistas, cultural experiences, and gastronomic pleasures. Whether you are a nature lover, a history buff, or simply searching for a calm vacation, Comox Valley offers a unique experience.

The Natural Beauty of Comox Valley.

Majestic mountains and scenic trails: The Beaufort Mountain Range, with its jagged peaks and verdant forests, provides a breathtaking background to the Comox Valley. These mountains provide a variety of hiking trails, ranging from short treks to difficult climbs.

Mount Washington: is a popular destination for both skiing and snowboarding in the winter, as well as hiking and mountain biking in the summer. The hikes offer amazing views of the valley and beyond. Strathcona Provincial Park, near to Mount Washington, contains some of Vancouver Island's most pristine wilderness areas, with trails leading to waterfalls, alpine meadows, and glacier lakes.

Forbidden Plateau: Previously a secret and holy spot for Indigenous peoples, it is today a popular trekking destination. The paths here, such as the Paradise Meadows Loop, provide spectacular views of the surrounding mountains and valleys, making it ideal for both casual hikers and experienced trekkers.

Pristine coastal waters

Comox Valley's shoreline is lined with sandy beaches, rocky shores, and sheltered coves, offering plenty of possibilities for water-based sports.

Goose Spit Park: This sandy spit stretches into Comox Harbour and is a popular area for swimming, picnics, and beachcombing. The park provides panoramic views of the Salish Sea and the surrounding mountains, making it an idyllic setting for a day out.

Seal Bay Nature Park: This coastal park has a network of pathways that lead through lush woodlands and along the seashore. The park is home to a variety of bird species and marine life, making it an excellent location for wildlife viewing. The peaceful surroundings and simple hikes make it ideal for families and wildlife enthusiasts.

Cultural and Historical Richness

Comox Valley is more than just natural beauty; it also has a rich cultural and historical legacy, which gives depth to its tranquil vistas.

Indigenous Heritage

The K'ómoks First Nation has occupied this area for thousands of years, and their cultural imprint may be seen across the valley.

I-Hos Gallery: This gallery, located on the K'ómoks First Nation grounds, displays the art and crafts of the Northwest Coast's indigenous peoples. Visitors can view a variety of artworks, from traditional carvings to contemporary sculptures, learning about the area's rich cultural past.

Ancient Petroglyphs: These ancient rock carvings, found throughout the region, provide insight into the lives and beliefs of Indigenous peoples. Visitors may reach sites like the Comox Lake Bluffs, which offer an interesting historical experience.

Colonial History and Heritage Sites

The European settlement of Comox Valley began in the mid-nineteenth century, and the region's history is carefully maintained in its cultural sites and museums.

Courtenay and District Museum: This museum takes visitors on a tour through the valley's history, beginning with dinosaurs and ending with the present. The paleontology exhibits, which feature fossils discovered in the area, are particularly remarkable, highlighting the region's rich prehistoric history.

Filberg Heritage Lodge and Park: Located in Comox, this historic lodge and park provides an insight into early twentieth-century life in the area. The wonderfully restored lodge, nestled among planted gardens and towering trees, offers a serene backdrop for a relaxing visit.

Outdoor Adventures and Activities

For those looking for adventure, Comox Valley has a wide range of outdoor activities to suit all levels of enthusiasm and expertise.

Kayaking and canoeing

The calm waters of Comox Harbour and adjacent rivers make the valley an ideal location for kayaking and canoeing.

Comox Harbour: Comox Harbour's protected waters are great for kayaking, with breathtaking views of the surrounding mountains and shoreline. Kayakers can explore the many inlets and bays, where they may see seals, otters, and other bird species.

Courtenay River: This lovely river runs through the center of the valley and is ideal for a relaxing paddle. The Courtenay River Estuary, where the river meets the sea, is a thriving environment full of animals, making it an ideal destination for nature lovers.

Cycling and Mountain Biking

The varied terrain of the Comox Valley offers good chances for both road and mountain biking.

Cumberland Forest: is well-known for its wide network of mountain bike paths, which cater to riders of all skill levels. The woodland is a biker's paradise, including tough single tracks as well as more accessible routes.

Comox Valley Parkway: This gorgeous route is ideal for road cyclists, with a combination of hard hills and calm descends. The parkway passes through some of the valley's most picturesque areas, offering breathtaking vistas and plenty of opportunities to stop and enjoy the scenery.

Culinary delights and local cuisine.

Comox Valley's lush soil and coastal waterways generate a plethora of fresh produce, seafood, and artisanal items, making it a culinary treat.

Farm-to-table Dining

The valley is home to various farms and markets, which supply local eateries with fresh, seasonal ingredients.

Locals Restaurant: This Courtenay-based restaurant focuses on farm-to-table eating, with a seasonal menu that highlights the best local ingredients. The dishes here reflect the valley's flavors, from fresh fish to locally grown veggies.

Cumberland Village Bakery: This lovely bakery in Cumberland serves a variety of tasty baked items prepared with locally sourced ingredients. It's the ideal place to grab a snack after a day of exploring the trails.

Wineries & Breweries

Comox Valley's temperate temperature makes it perfect for viticulture and brewing, and the region is home to several notable wineries and artisan breweries.

40 Knots Winery: Located in Comox, this winery offers a wide range of wines that reflect the region's distinct terroir. Visitors can enjoy tastings, excursions, and activities surrounded by magnificent vineyards.

Gladstone Brewing Co.: Courtenay's craft brewery serves a variety of beers brewed on-site, including zesty IPAs and creamy stouts. The brewery's taproom is a favorite hangout for both locals and visitors, offering a comfortable setting to enjoy a pint and some local fare.

Annual Events and Festivals.

Comox Valley holds several events and festivals throughout the year to celebrate its culture, wildlife, and community spirit.

Filberg Festival: This annual arts and crafts festival, held in the scenic Filberg Park, highlights the work of local artisans and craftspeople. The festival includes live music, food vendors, and a variety of activities, making it a family-friendly event that attracts people from all over.

Comox Valley Farmers' Market: The Comox Valley Farmers' Market, open year-round, is a monument to the region's agricultural richness. The market sells a wide variety of local products, including fresh produce, meats, artisanal cheeses, and baked goods. It's a must-see for anyone wishing to sample the flavors of the valley.

Vancouver Island Music Festival: This popular music festival, held in Courtenay, draws a diverse range of performers from around the world. The event includes several stages, workshops, and food vendors, resulting in a lively setting that celebrates music and community.

Wellness & Relaxation

Comox Valley provides a variety of wellness experiences that take advantage of the region's natural beauty and tranquility.

Spas & Retreats

Kingfisher Oceanside Resort & Spa: This magnificent resort, located on the banks of the Salish Sea, offers a variety of spa treatments to help you rest and recharge. The spa's distinctive Pacific Mist Hydropath offers a unique experience that combines hydrotherapy with breathtaking ocean views.

Crown Isle Resort & Golf Community: This Courtenay resort provides a tranquil atmosphere for relaxation, along with a world-class golf course, exquisite accommodations, and a full-service spa. It's an excellent choice for people seeking to unwind in a gorgeous setting.

Yoga and Wellness Studio

Comox Valley's serene climate makes it excellent for yoga and wellness practices.

Serenity Lodge Retreat: Located in a peaceful forested setting, this retreat center provides yoga lessons, meditation sessions, and wellness programs. It's the ideal spot to disconnect and reconnect with nature and oneself.

Courtenay Massage Therapy: This wellness center in Courtenay provides a variety of therapeutic massage therapies to help visitors attain physical and mental well-being. Professional therapists offer personalized treatments in a relaxing setting.

Comox Valley, with its breathtaking natural beauty, rich cultural past, and many outdoor and wellness activities, represents nature and serenity. Whether you're hiking in the gorgeous mountains, kayaking along the pristine shoreline, learning about the rich history, or enjoying local cuisine, Comox Valley provides a peaceful and enriching experience. Its combination of natural beauty and cultural depth makes it an ideal destination for anyone seeking both adventure and relaxation. As you explore the valley, you will come across a location where nature and community coexist together, allowing you to immerse yourself in the beauty and calm of this unique environment.

Port Hardy: Gateway to the Wilderness.

Port Hardy, on Vancouver Island's northern tip, embodies the region's rugged beauty and daring attitude. Port Hardy, known as the gateway to the outdoors, provides a distinct blend of untamed scenery, a rich cultural past, and outdoor activities. This book delves deeply into what makes Port Hardy a unique destination, from its natural beauties and fauna to its cultural attractions and recreational activities.

Natural Wonders and Scenic Beauty

Pristine Landscape: Port Hardy is bordered by some of Vancouver Island's most beautiful and diversified natural scenery. The village serves as a gateway to the extensive wilderness areas that define the island's northern region.

Cape Scott Provincial Park: is a must-see for visitors seeking secluded, untouched beauty. Cape Scott, with its rocky coastal cliffs, beautiful beaches, and lush forests, is a hiking and nature lover's paradise. The Cape Scott Trail, which leads to the landmark lighthouse, provides stunning views of the Pacific Ocean and an opportunity to appreciate the raw beauty of the coastline.

San Josef Bay: accessible via a reasonably simple hike from Cape Scott Provincial Park, is well-known for its spectacular sea stacks and clean beaches. The bay's remote setting makes it excellent for camping, picnics, and discovering tide pools filled with marine life.

Wildlife Viewing

Port Hardy is an excellent site for viewing a variety of species in their natural surroundings. The region's different ecosystems sustain a wide range of animals, making it a wildlife lover's dream.

Whale Watching: Several whale species, including grey whales, humpbacks, and orcas, use the waters around Port Hardy as a migration path. Whale-watching trips allow you to see these amazing creatures up close, as well as other marine species like dolphins and sea lions.

Bear Watching: Both black and grizzly bears live in the forests and waterways surrounding Port Hardy. Guided tours offer safe and educational bear-viewing experiences, with a focus on the bears' salmon fishing activities throughout the spawning season.

Bird Watching: The area is also a bird watcher's paradise, with many different types of seabirds, waterfowl, and raptors. The estuaries, coastal areas, and woodlands surrounding Port Hardy provide good opportunity to observe bald eagles, herons, and a variety of other bird species.

Cultural Heritage and Community Spirit

The Kwakiutl First Nation's customs, as well as the town's past as a fishing and logging community, provide the foundation of Port Hardy's cultural legacy.

Indigenous culture: The Kwakiutl First Nation has been in the northern section of Vancouver Island for thousands of years, and its rich cultural legacy can be seen in the art, traditions, and community life in Port Hardy.

The U'mista Cultural Centre: located in adjacent Alert Bay, displays an extensive collection of Indigenous artifacts including ceremonial masks, regalia, and carvings. The center is dedicated to preserving and educating Kwakiutl culture, with exhibits, cultural performances, and educational programs.

Totem Poles: The town and neighboring areas include several remarkable totem poles that convey stories about the Kwakiutl people's history and beliefs. These totems are not only stunning pieces of art but also significant cultural icons.

Historic Sites

Port Hardy's past as a fishing and logging hub has left an indelible mark that can be explored at its historical sites and museums.

The Port Hardy Museum: provides a peek into the town's history, with displays on early settlers, the forestry and fishing industries, and local Indigenous culture. Artifacts, pictures, and interactive displays make it an invaluable resource for learning about the region's past.

The Quatse Salmon Stewardship Centre: focuses on the conservation and education of salmon and their ecosystems. Visitors can learn about salmon life cycles, the significance of sustainable fishing practices, and attempts to safeguard these critical species. The center also offers an educational walk and a hatchery tour.

Outdoor adventure and recreational activities.

Port Hardy is a paradise for outdoor enthusiasts, with a diverse choice of activities catering to all levels of adventure and experience.

Hiking & Trail Adventures

The various geography surrounding Port Hardy offers excellent hiking possibilities, ranging from seaside treks to tough mountain trails.

North Coast Trail: This steep trail is one of the most difficult and rewarding climbs on Vancouver Island. The North Coast Trail, which runs for 43 kilometers through Cape Scott Provincial Park, features breathtaking coastal views, secluded beaches, and dense forests. The trek is perfect for experienced hikers seeking adventure in a natural forest setting.

The Marble River Trail: is a more accessible option that follows the picturesque Marble River through thick woodlands and along its banks. The path is well-known for its salmon streams and provides excellent chances for fishing, animal observation, and photography.

Fishing and Boating

The waters near Port Hardy are loaded with fish, making it an ideal fishing location. There are several fishing options, ranging from freshwater rivers to the open ocean.

Sport Fishing: The region is well-known for its great sport fishing prospects, which include salmon, halibut, and other species. Charter services offer guided fishing expeditions ranging from day excursions to multi-day experiences. The competent guides assure a successful and pleasurable visit.

Kayaking and canoeing: Port Hardy's sheltered bays and inlets are ideal for these activities. Paddlers can explore the shoreline, find hidden coves, and enjoy the tranquil surroundings. Kayak rentals and guided tours are provided for both new and seasoned paddlers.

Diving and Snorkelling

The chilly, clear seas of Port Hardy provide some of the best diving and snorkeling opportunities in the Pacific Northwest.

God's Pocket Marine Provincial Park: Located close to the coast, this marine park is a popular diving site. Underwater landscapes include bright coral reefs, kelp forests, and a variety of marine life. Dive operators in Port Hardy provide trips to God's Pocket, which include all you need for an unforgettable underwater experience.

Browning Pass: Known for its outstanding marine life, Browning Pass is a popular dive and snorkel destination. The area's powerful currents sustain a diverse environment, including colorful anemones, sponges, and many fish species.

Culinary delights and local cuisine.

Port Hardy's culinary culture reflects the area's bountiful natural resources, with an emphasis on fresh fish and locally produced products.

Fresh seafood: Because of the town's coastal position, fresh seafood is always available, and it is a popular item on local menus.

Seafood Restaurants: Many restaurants in Port Hardy specialize in seafood, serving dishes created with fresh fish, shellfish, and other marine delicacies. Popular restaurants, such as the Quarterdeck Inn & Marina Resort, offer riverside dining with harbor views and a menu including the greatest seafood in the region.

Local Markets: For those who prefer to prepare their meals, the town's markets and fishmongers sell fresh, locally caught seafood. The Fisherman's Wharf is an excellent spot to buy directly from the source, where fishermen sell their daily catches.

Farm-to-table Dining

In addition to seafood, Port Hardy's culinary culture features farm-to-table cuisine, with restaurants acquiring products from nearby farms and producers.

Local Farms: The fertile lands surrounding Port Hardy support a diverse range of farms that provide fresh vegetables, fruits, and meats. Farmers' markets and farm stands are excellent places to find these locally produced items, which are also prominently featured in the town's eateries.

Artisan Producers: The region is home to several artisan producers, who sell everything from handcrafted cheeses to locally brewed beer. These products are available in local shops and restaurants, offering a sense of the region's workmanship and culinary innovation.

Annual Events and Festivals.

Port Hardy's community spirit is exemplified by its annual events and festivals, which honor the region's culture, legacy, and natural beauty.

Filomi Days: Filomi Days, one of Port Hardy's most popular events, commemorates the town's history and sense of community. The celebration includes a procession, live music, food vendors, and a variety of family-friendly activities. It's an excellent opportunity to learn about local culture while also having a good time.

BC Marine Trails Network Association Festival.

This festival commemorates the wide network of marine trails along the British Columbia coast. The event will feature paddling tours, workshops, and presentations on marine conservation and outdoor leisure. It's an ideal event for people who enjoy kayaking and exploring the coastal wilderness.

Winterfest: Winterfest, which takes place during the holiday season, brings together the community through festive activities such as a Christmas market, ice skating, and holiday-themed events. The festival fosters a warm and friendly environment while celebrating the spirit of the season.

Port Hardy, with its breathtaking natural settings, rich cultural past, and diverse choice of outdoor activities, certainly lives up to its status as the entrance to the wilderness. Port Hardy provides a unique and enriching experience, whether you're exploring the rugged coastline, viewing wildlife in their natural habitats, learning about the town's history, or dining on fresh local food. Its combination of adventure, tranquility, and community spirit makes it an ideal place for people looking to reconnect with nature and enjoy Vancouver Island's wild beauty. As you immerse yourself in everything Port Hardy has to offer, you will discover a spot where the wilderness meets the sea, resulting in an extraordinary journey.

Outdoor Activities on Vancouver Island

Vancouver Island is an outdoor enthusiast's dream, thanks to its diverse landscapes and magnificent natural beauty. From steep mountain hikes and quiet seaside roads to adrenaline-pumping biking routes and tranquil kayaking waters, the island provides a plethora of opportunities to immerse oneself in nature. This guide delves into the numerous outdoor adventures accessible on Vancouver Island, offering thorough information on the best places for hiking, biking, kayaking, and other activities.

Hiking: Exploring Vancouver Island on Foot.

Vancouver Island is well-known for its large network of hiking routes, which cater to all levels of experience. Whether you want a strenuous walk across rugged terrain or a stroll along the seaside, the island has something for everyone.

Iconic Hiking Trails.

The West Coast Trail: is one of Canada's most recognized hiking trails, stretching 75 kilometers along the island's southwestern edge. This difficult trail leads hikers through lush forests, around rocky shorelines, and over suspension bridges. It's a trek that requires preparation and endurance, but it rewards hikers with breathtaking views and a profound sense of accomplishment.

The Juan de Fuca Marine Trail: is a slightly less challenging alternative to the West Coast Trail, stretching 47 kilometers along the island's west coast. The walk provides breathtaking ocean views, lush jungle trails, and the opportunity to see wildlife including whales and sea lions. Mystic Beach, with its breathtaking waterfall, and Botanical Beach, with its one-of-a-kind tide pools, are must-sees along the walk.

Mount Albert Edward: Located in Strathcona Provincial Park, this trail climbs to one of the island's highest points. The walk up Mount Albert Edward is strenuous, but the panoramic views from the summit, which include the Comox Glacier and the surrounding peaks, make it a worthy undertaking. The trail passes through a variety of scenery, including alpine meadows and steep slopes.

Family-Friendly Hikes

Elk Falls Provincial Park: This park near Campbell River is home to the stunning Elk Falls, which plunges into a deep canyon. The park has well-kept trails suited for all ages, including a suspension bridge that affords a spectacular view of the falls. The pathways wind through old-growth forests, providing both spectacular views and educational possibilities.

Goldstream Provincial Park: located just outside Victoria, is well-known for its stunning waterfalls, historic woods, and vigorous salmon flows. The park's easy routes, such as the short walk to Niagara Falls, make it ideal for families. The park also has an interpretive center where visitors may learn about the local plants and animals.

Remote and Difficult Hikes

Nootka Trail: For those looking for a true wilderness experience, the Nootka Trail on Nootka Island provides a lonely and rough trip. The trail is roughly 35 kilometers long and features a combination of beach strolling, forest trails, and river crossings. Hikers can discover stunning beaches, old First Nations sites, and other fauna along the path.

The Cape Scott Trail: travels to the Cape Scott Lighthouse on Vancouver Island's northern tip, passing through rugged and desolate terrain. The trail winds through lush jungles, over swampy terrain, and along windswept beaches. It's a strenuous walk that provides seclusion and the opportunity to see the island's wild beauty.

Biking: Exploring the Island on Two Wheels.

Vancouver Island is a cyclist's paradise, with a variety of bicycling routes ranging from leisurely rides through gorgeous countryside to challenging mountain bike paths.

Road Cycling

Lochside Regional Path: This popular multi-use path connects Victoria to Swartz Bay, encompassing 29 kilometers of scenic vistas. The trail is largely level and accessible to bikers of all ages and abilities. It runs past farmlands, shorelines, and picturesque settlements, providing for a pleasant and scenic trip.

Cowichan Valley Trail: The Cowichan Valley Trail, part of the Trans Canada Trail, is 122 kilometers long and includes both paved and unpaved sections. The walk contains the magnificent Kinsol Trestle, which is one of the world's tallest wooden trestle bridges. Cyclists can take leisurely rides through forests, vineyards, and along riverbanks.

Mountain Biking

Cumberland Forest is well-known for its wide network of mountain bike paths, which cater to riders of all skill levels. The trails range from flowing single tracks to difficult downhill rides, winding through lush forests and past historic mining remnants. Cumberland is a mountain biking culture hotspot, complete with bike stores, cafes, and a friendly riding environment.

Mount Washington Bike Park: During the summer, Mount Washington Alpine Resort transforms into a mountain-riding hotspot. The bike park has lift-accessed tracks for all ability levels, from beginner-friendly routes to challenging downhill courses. The park's paths provide breathtaking mountain views and exhilarating descents.

Gravel and Adventure Riding

Great Trail (Trans Canada Trail): The Great Trail's stretch on Vancouver Island offers excellent gravel and adventure riding. The pathway crosses a variety of terrains, including forest paths, logging roads, and coastal routes. Riders can go on multi-day backpacking treks in rural places, camping along the route.

Bamfield route: For those seeking a more distant adventure, the gravel route to Bamfield on the island's west coast is both demanding and scenic. The path runs through forests, along rivers, and connects to the Pacific Rim National Park Reserve. It's a tough yet rewarding route for seasoned adventure cyclists.

Water Activities: Kayaking, Canoeing, and More.

The coastal seas, lakes, and rivers of Vancouver Island provide ideal conditions for kayaking, canoeing, and other water-based activities. Paddlers can explore tranquil lakes, and cross-twisting rivers, and find secret coves along the shore.

Sea kayaking

The Broken Group Islands, located in Barkley Sound, are a kayaker's paradise. This archipelago of over 100 islands and islets boasts calm waters, diverse fauna, and scenic beaches. Paddlers can camp at specified locations, discover historic Indigenous sites, and relax in this protected area.

Clayoquot Sound: This UNESCO Biosphere Reserve near Tofino offers an excellent environment for sea kayaking. The area's ecosystems are diverse, including old-growth rainforests, tidal flats, and secluded beaches. Kayakers can see whales, sea otters, and a variety of bird species while exploring the complicated canals.

Lake and River Paddling

Cowichan River: This river is popular for canoeing and kayaking, with a combination of calm and hard rapids. The Cowichan River Provincial Park offers access points, camping facilities, and attractive picnic and swimming areas. The river's beautiful waters and natural environs make it a favorite among paddlers.

Great Central Lake, located near Port Alberni, is one of the island's largest freshwater lakes. The lake's tranquil waters are ideal for kayaking and canoeing, with plenty of bays and coves to explore. The lake also serves as the beginning point for the strenuous Della Falls climb.

Stand Up Paddleboarding (SUP)

The tranquil waters of Victoria's Inner Harbour are excellent for stand-up paddleboarding. While gliding around the harbor, paddlers can take in views of the city's historic sites, including the Parliament Buildings and Empress Hotel. Rentals and guided tours are provided for both novice and experienced paddlers.

Comox Lake: This glacially fed lake in Courtenay provides ideal conditions for stand-up paddleboarding. The lake's pristine waters and attractive surroundings make it ideal for a relaxed paddle. The nearby town of Cumberland offers amenities and access to additional outdoor activities.

Other Outdoor Adventures

Aside from hiking, riding, and paddling, Vancouver Island has a variety of other outdoor activities to suit a wide range of interests and adventure levels.

Rock climbing and bouldering

Horne Lake Caves Provincial Park: This park near Qualicum Beach is well-known for both its caves and its rock climbing opportunities. The limestone cliffs provide routes for climbers of all abilities. Guided cave tours offer a one-of-a-kind underground journey, with fascinating formations and underground rivers to discover.

Mount Wells Regional Park: located near Victoria, is known for its granite cliffs, which are popular among rock climbers. The climbing routes range from beginner to intermediate, with spectacular views of the surrounding area from the summit.

Caving

Horne Lake Caves: The large cave system at Horne Lake offers an exciting trip for caving aficionados. Guided tours range from simple excursions through enormous caverns to more difficult spelunking expeditions that require crawling through tiny corridors and scaling underground waterfalls.

Upana Caves: Located near the Gold River, Upana Caves are a collection of easily accessible caverns for exploring. The caves have distinctive structures and offer a cool escape throughout the summer months. The routes leading to the caves are well-marked and ideal for families.

Wildlife safaris

Grizzly Bear Tours: Guided tours of Vancouver Island's northern districts allow visitors to see grizzly bears in their native habitat. Tours are often conducted in isolated wilderness locations accessible by boat or floatplane. These safaris offer a rare opportunity to see bears fishing for salmon and socializing in the wild.

Whale Watching: The waters surrounding Vancouver Island are famous for whale watching. Tours departing from Victoria, Tofino, and Port Hardy provide the opportunity to witness orcas, humpbacks, and grey whales. The cruises frequently feature educational comments about marine life and conservation efforts.

Vancouver Island is a treasure mine of outdoor adventures, with something for everyone, from casual nature lovers to extreme adventurers. Whether you're hiking through ancient forests, biking along gorgeous routes, canoeing in tranquil waterways, or exploring underground caves, the island's various landscapes and rich natural beauty promise amazing adventures.

Each excursion not only connects you with nature but also allows you to learn about the region's rich ecological and cultural legacy. As you embark on your outdoor excursions on Vancouver Island, you'll discover that every trail, wave, and vista beckons you to explore and connect with the raw beauty of nature.

Whale Watching and Wildlife Tours on Vancouver Island.

Vancouver Island is a top destination for wildlife aficionados, providing an unequaled opportunity to see some of the most spectacular creatures on the globe. From the breathtaking sight of orcas gliding through the water to the joyful antics of sea otters and the majesty of bald eagles soaring overhead, the island offers a front-row ticket to nature's performance. This book digs into the diverse possibilities of whale watching and wildlife tours on Vancouver Island, including what tourists may anticipate, the best times to visit, and how to make the most of these memorable experiences.

The Spectacle of Whale Watching

Whale watching on Vancouver Island is a transforming experience that draws visitors from all around the world. The waters around the island are teeming with marine life, including numerous species of whales.

Types of Whales

Orcas (Killer Whales): Perhaps the most recognizable of all, orcas can be seen all year round on Vancouver Island. There are two types: resident orcas, which predominantly eat fish, and transient orcas, which hunt marine animals. Resident pods are commonly seen in the waters off Victoria and the southern Gulf Islands.

Humpback whales: known for their stunning breaches and long, complex songs, are most commonly sighted between May and October. During the summer, these giants move to the nutrient-rich waters of Vancouver Island to feed.

Grey whales: are frequently seen as they migrate between Mexico and the Arctic. The ideal times to watch grey whales are in the spring when they travel north, and in the autumn, when they migrate south.

Minke Whales: Though smaller and more elusive than other species, minke whales can be seen on

Vancouver Island, especially during the summer months.

Best Places for Whale Watching

Victoria: The capital city is a popular destination for whale-watching cruises. The waters surrounding Victoria are ideal for observing orcas, humpbacks, and grey whales. Companies such as Prince of Whales and Orca Spirit Adventures provide a variety of trips departing from Victoria's Inner Harbour.

Tofino and Ucluelet: These West Coast cities offer access to the abundant marine ecosystems of Clayoquot Sound and Barkley Sound. Tours departing from Tofino and Ucluelet frequently meet grey whales, humpback whales, and orcas. Jamie's Whaling Station and Ocean Outfitters are popular establishments in the region.

Campbell River: located on the island's east coast, is another great place to start your whale-watching adventure. Orcas, humpbacks, and the occasional minke whale have all been spotted in the vicinity.

Tours here frequently involve the thrill of passing through the picturesque Discovery Passage.

Wildlife Tours: Beyond the Whales

While whale viewing is a popular activity, Vancouver Island's wildlife tours provide much more, highlighting the island's unique ecosystems and plentiful fauna.

Marine Wildlife Tours

Sea Otters: These endearing critters are frequently seen floating on their backs in the kelp beds around the island. The west coast, notably around Tofino and Ucluelet, provides an excellent opportunity to observe sea otters in their native environment.

Seals and Sea Lions: Harbour seals and Steller sea lions are frequently spotted on the island's beaches and rocky outcrops. Whale-watching trips frequently include views of these marine creatures, particularly in places like the Race Rocks Ecological Reserve in Victoria.

Porpoises and Dolphins: Dall's porpoises and Pacific white-sided dolphins are noted for their lively behavior and can be seen surfing boats' bow waves. These fast-moving cetaceans are entertaining to observe and frequently bring an element of surprise to marine tours.

Bird Watching

Vancouver Island is a birdwatcher's dream, with a varied range of bird species living in its many settings.

Bald Eagles: These gorgeous birds are commonly seen on Vancouver Island. They can be observed perched in lofty trees, soaring overhead, or fishing near the coast. The Campbell River area, as well as the estuaries near Comox and Courtenay, are popular eagle-watching locations.

Seabirds: Puffins, murres, and auklets can be found along the island's coastline and in the offshore waters. Bird-watching trips frequently visit Clayoquot

Sound and the Broken Group Islands, which are both protected areas.

Migratory Birds: The island's wetlands and estuary are key stopovers for migratory birds. The greatest times to watch shorebirds and waterfowl are during their migration seasons in the spring and autumn. The Pacific Rim National Park Reserve and the Cowichan Estuary are outstanding birdwatching destinations.

Plan Your Wildlife Adventure

To get the most out of your whale watching and wildlife excursion on Vancouver Island, proper planning is required. Here are some suggestions and considerations for a wonderful encounter.

Selecting the Right Tour Operator

Research and Reviews: Look for tour providers with a good reputation and excellent feedback. Check internet sites such as TripAdvisor and Google Reviews for feedback from past visitors.

Eco-friendly procedures: Choose operators who are dedicated to sustainable and ethical wildlife viewing procedures. These companies adhere to criteria that minimize disruption to animals and their environments.

Safety and Comfort: Ensure that the tour operator provides well-maintained vessels outfitted with safety equipment. Knowledgeable guides and naturalists may substantially enhance your experience by explaining the behavior and ecology of the creatures you see.

Best Time to Go

Seasonality: Different species appear more frequently at different periods of the year. For example, orcas can be seen all year, but humpback whales are more abundant from May to October, and grey whales are most visible during their migrations in the spring and autumn.

Time of Day: Early morning and late afternoon trips frequently provide the finest light for photography and may coincide with feeding times for some species, boosting the likelihood of encounters.

What to bring.

Dress in layers to adapt to changing weather conditions. Waterproof coats and trousers are important, especially on boat journeys.

Binoculars and Cameras: Bring binoculars for a closer look at distant species and a camera with a good zoom lens to capture special moments.

Snacks and Water: While some tours supply refreshments, it's a good idea to carry your own, especially on longer trips.

Conservation and Responsible Tourism.

Participating in whale watching and wildlife tours on Vancouver Island allows you to support conservation efforts while also learning about the importance of protecting these ecosystems.

Marine conservation initiatives

Research and Education: Many tour operators work with marine scientists and conservationists to conduct research and educate the public on marine species. Your involvement helps to fund these critical projects.

Protected zones: Visiting marine protected zones helps to save key habitats. These areas provide safe havens for marine life and are critical for biodiversity conservation.

Ethical Wildlife Viewing.

Respectful Distance: Always keep a respectful distance from wildlife to avoid stress and disruption. Operators who adhere to ethical rules ensure that excursions are performed in a way that prioritizes the welfare of the animals.

Follow the Leave No Trace principles: by not disrupting habitats, correctly disposing of rubbish, and minimizing your ecological imprint while on trips.

Unique Wildlife Experiences

Aside from standard excursions, Vancouver Island has several unique wildlife encounters that allow for more immersion and interaction with nature.

Kayak and paddleboard Wildlife Tours: A guided kayak or paddleboard excursion provides a more intimate and environmentally responsible approach to exploring the island's seas. These cruises provide a calm and low-impact way to approach marine species, frequently resulting in closer and more personal interactions.

Wilderness Camping and Guided Hikes: Combining animal viewing with backcountry camping or guided treks might result in a deeper, more immersive experience. Outfitters such as West Coast Expeditions provide multi-day kayaking and camping experiences with the opportunity to observe marine and terrestrial wildlife up close.

Indigenous Cultural Tours: Indigenous-led tours provide a unique look at the island's fauna and ecosystems. These excursions frequently combine traditional knowledge and storytelling, allowing visitors to have a better appreciation of the land and its residents' cultural value. Companies such as Sea Wolf Adventures and Homalco Wildlife & Cultural Tours offer enriching experiences that combine wildlife watching and cultural education.

Whale watching and wildlife tours on Vancouver Island are more than just activities; they are transformative experiences that deepen tourists' connections to the natural world. The island's diverse marine and terrestrial habitats, together with responsible and educated tour operators, provide exceptional opportunities to see and enjoy animals.

From the thrill of seeing orcas breach the surface to the serene awe of watching eagles soar overhead, these encounters leave an indelible impact and build a greater respect for the need to conserve and maintain these extraordinary places. Whether you're a seasoned wildlife enthusiast or a first-time visitor, Vancouver Island's whale watching and wildlife tours guarantee an instructive and inspirational trip, providing a window into nature's beauties that few locations can match.

Indigenous Cultural Experiences on Vancouver Island.

Vancouver Island is rich in natural beauty and cultural heritage, particularly that of its Indigenous peoples. The island is home to various Indigenous cultures, each with its unique traditions, dialects, and history. Engaging in Indigenous cultural experiences on Vancouver Island provides visitors with a profound opportunity to connect with the land and its original stewards while learning about ancient practices, modern life, and the deep spiritual connections that define these communities. This book discusses the various opportunities to experience Indigenous culture on Vancouver Island, including guided tours, cultural centers, festivals, and traditional art.

Understanding Indigenous Heritage

Vancouver Island's Indigenous peoples include the Coast Salish, Nuu-chah-nulth, and Kwakwaka'wakw tribes. Each of these communities has a rich cultural past that is intricately linked to the natural environment. Their traditions, legends, and rituals demonstrate a great appreciation for the land and water, which have supported them for millennia.

The Coast Salish People: The Coast Salish peoples, who live in the south of the island, include the Cowichan, Tsawout, Tsartlip, and other groups. Their culture is characterized by complex weaving, elaborate ceremonies, and a strong connection to the land and water.

The Nuu-chah-nulth Nation: The Nuu-chah-nulth people, who live on the island's west coast, are well-known for their whaling traditions, ornate carvings, and rich oral histories. They have a strong bond with the ocean, which is essential to their cultural and spiritual lives.

The Kwakwaka'wakw people: The Kwakwaka'wakw people live in the northern section of Vancouver Island and are known for their potlatch celebrations, totem poles, and expressive masks. Their culture focuses on community, storytelling, and the natural world.

Immersive Cultural Tours

Homalco Wildlife and Cultural Tours: Homalco Wildlife & Cultural Tours, based near Campbell River, provides a unique blend of wildlife watching and cultural instruction. Visitors can take guided trips to explore traditional regions, learn about the importance of local flora and fauna, and experience Homalco cultural traditions. Highlights include bear-viewing tours and engaging cultural demonstrations.

Sea Wolf Adventures: Sea Wolf Adventures, guided by Kwakwaka'wakw people, offers trips that mix animal watching and cultural instruction. Departing from Port McNeill, these trips provide an intimate look at the region's natural and cultural legacy, including visits to old village sites and storytelling sessions that bring Kwakwaka'wakw history and stories to life.

Tsa-kwa-Luten Lodge: Tsa-Kwa-Luten Lodge, located on Quadra Island, provides a culturally intensive experience in a picturesque natural setting. The lodge itself exemplifies Coast Salish architecture and design, and it serves as a platform for exploring the island's cultural and natural highlights. Guests can enjoy guided excursions, traditional cuisine, and cultural entertainment.

Cultural Centres and Museums

U'mista Cultural Centre: The U'mista Cultural Centre, in Alert Bay, is dedicated to preserving and presenting Kwakwaka'wakw culture. The center's exhibits feature a rare collection of potlatch regalia that was returned after being confiscated during the potlatch ban in the early twentieth century. Visitors can learn about the Kwakwaka'wakw people's history, art, and traditions through interactive displays and educational programs.

Quw'utsun Cultural and Conference Centre: In Duncan, the Quw'utsun Cultural and Conference Centre offers an in-depth look at Cowichan culture. The center houses traditional weaving, carving, and other arts exhibits, as well as musical and dance performances. Guided tours provide insight into Cowichan history and the importance of the land and waterways in their culture.

The Nuu-chah-nulth Cultural Centre: This center, located in Ucluelet, celebrates the Nuu-chah-nulth people's rich past. The exhibits feature ancient whaling operations, artistic carvings, and deep spiritual links to the ocean. The center also provides educational programs and workshops in traditional crafts and storytelling.

Traditional Art and Craft

Carving & Totem Poles: Carving is an integral part of Indigenous traditions on Vancouver Island. Totem poles, masks, and other carvings are more than just creative expressions; they are also historical records and spiritual symbols.

Art Galleries and Studios: Many Indigenous artisans on Vancouver Island open their studios to the public, allowing visitors to observe the carving process and purchase unique items. The Alcheringa Gallery in Victoria and the Eagle Aerie Gallery in Tofino display a diverse spectrum of Indigenous art, from traditional carvings to contemporary works.

Totem Pole Tours: Guided tours, such as those conducted in Alert Bay and Duncan, provide a thorough understanding of the significance of totem poles. These excursions explain the history and symbolism associated with the poles, as well as the cultural background in which they were formed.

Weaving and Textile: Weaving is another major art form, especially among Coast Salish peoples. Weaving's unique patterns and techniques have been passed down for generations.

Weaving Workshops: Some cultural centers and artists host workshops where visitors can learn the fundamentals of traditional weaving. These hands-on experiences help you appreciate the talent and cultural relevance of this art form.

Cedar bark weaving is a traditional technique used in many Indigenous cultures to create baskets, headgear, and other products. Workshops on cedar bark weaving teach about the gathering and processing of the bark, as well as weaving techniques.

Festivals and ceremonies

Participating in festivals and rituals provides an excellent opportunity to learn about the current culture of Vancouver Island's Indigenous peoples.

Pacific Rim Whale Festival: This celebration, held annually in March, commemorates the return of grey whales to the waters surrounding Vancouver Island. The Nuu-chah-nulth people will give a range of cultural demonstrations, including storytelling, traditional dances, and art displays. It's a bright celebration that emphasizes the Nuu-chah-nulth's close bond with the ocean.

The Tofino Lantern Festival: This neighborhood celebration, usually in August, includes a stunning display of handcrafted lanterns. The festival features workshops taught by local Indigenous artists who teach attendees how to make lanterns based on traditional motifs. The celebration finishes with a lantern parade, creating a wonderful ambiance that honors light and creativity.

The Alert Bay Sea Festival: Seafest is a summer event in Alert Bay that features cultural performances, traditional cuisine, and family-friendly activities. The celebration celebrates the Kwakwaka'wakw people's marine heritage, including canoe races, seafood feasts, and cultural demonstrations.

Cuisine and Traditional Foods

Exploring the traditional food of Vancouver Island's Indigenous peoples is a delightful and educational experience. Many meals draw on the region's plentiful natural resources, such as seafood, animals, and wild flora.

Traditional feasts: Salmon Bakes: Salmon is a staple food for many Indigenous communities on Vancouver Island. Traditional salmon bakes, which are commonly held at festivals and community gatherings, provide a taste of this classic meal. Salmon is generally cooked over an open fire on cedar planks, giving it a rich, smokey flavor.

Potlatch Feasts: While not open to the public, knowing the significance of the potlatch feast can provide insight into Indigenous culture. These meetings involve the exchange of food, storytelling, and gifts, which strengthens communal relationships and social institutions.

Indigenous-inspired restaurants

Kekuli Café: with sites in Duncan and beyond, serves a menu influenced by traditional Indigenous cuisine. The café is well-known for its bannock, a sort of frybread that is popular in many Indigenous communities and comes with a variety of toppings and fillings.

Salmon n' Bannock Bistro: located in Victoria, delivers contemporary meals with traditional Indigenous flavors. The menu includes locally derived delicacies such as wild game, seafood, and berries, cooked using both modern and traditional methods.

Learning & Educational Experiences

Educational programs and experiences offer in-depth insights into the history, culture, and contemporary lives of Vancouver Island's Indigenous people.

Storytelling Sessions: Storytelling is an essential part of Indigenous culture, utilized to pass down information, history, and values. Many cultural centers and tours provide storytelling sessions in which guests can hear traditional stories and learn about their meanings and relevance.

Educational Workshops: Workshops on traditional crafts, languages, and cultural practices provide hands-on learning experiences. These workshops, sometimes given by knowledgeable community members, provide a more in-depth understanding of the skills and knowledge passed down through generations.

School and Community Programs: Many Indigenous cultural centers provide programs for schools and community organizations that teach about Indigenous culture and history. These programs frequently contain interactive aspects such as craft projects, storytelling, and performances, making them enjoyable and educational for people of all ages.

Supporting Indigenous Communities

Engaging in Indigenous cultural experiences on Vancouver Island is not only rewarding but also helps to preserve and perpetuate these cultures.

Ethical Tourism: Choosing tours and activities led by Indigenous guides and run by Indigenous-owned businesses ensures that your trip supports the local community. It also ensures a more genuine and courteous encounter.

Supporting Indigenous Artists and Craftspeople: Buying art, crafts, and products from Indigenous artists and businesses benefits their livelihoods while also preserving traditional skills and knowledge. Look for galleries, marketplaces, and shops that sell genuine Indigenous art and artisans.

Advocate for Indigenous Rights and Land Stewardship: Learning about Indigenous people's history and present concerns, as well as campaigning for their rights and land stewardship, is a vital way to offer support. Many cultural centers and organizations offer information on how visitors can get involved and help these causes.

Indigenous cultural experiences on Vancouver Island provide a profound and fascinating opportunity to connect with the land and its original inhabitants. Immersive tours and educational seminars, as well as festivals and gastronomic pleasures, provide several chances to learn about and celebrate the Coast Salish, Nuu-chah-nulth, and Kwakwaka'wakw peoples' rich cultural legacy. These encounters not only provide insight into old customs and modern living but also help to preserve and sustain these dynamic civilizations. Exploring Vancouver Island through the prism of its Indigenous past can help you appreciate the land, its history, and the tenacious communities that still live here.

Museums and Historical Sites on Vancouver Island

Vancouver Island, with its rich tapestry of history and culture, is home to numerous museums and historical sites that provide in-depth insights into the past. These institutions and sites shed light on the lives of Indigenous peoples, early European settlers, and the varied populations that have defined the island's history.

Museums and historical sites on Vancouver Island offer people of all ages and interests, interactive displays, ancient artifacts, historic structures, and educational programs. This guide delves into some of the most prominent locales, explaining what makes each one distinctive and worth visiting.

Royal BC Museum, Victoria

The Royal British Columbia Museum, located in the center of Victoria, is one of Canada's most prestigious cultural organizations. Its broad collections and engaging exhibits provide an in-depth look at British Columbia's nature and human history.

Indigenous Collections: The museum's First Peoples Gallery delves deeply into the diverse cultures and history of British Columbia's Indigenous peoples. Visitors can learn about Indigenous life in the past and present through exhibits such as elaborate carvings, ceremonial regalia, and a rebuilt traditional longhouse.

Natural History: The Natural History Gallery displays the varied ecosystems of British Columbia. Highlights include life-sized dioramas of local fauna, a model of coastal rainforest, and an ice age exhibit containing woolly mammoth relics.

Modern history: The Modern History Gallery explores the colonial and modern centuries, featuring displays on the fur trade, gold rush, and urban growth. Interactive displays and artifacts bring to life the stories of those who shaped the province's past.

Nanaimo Museum

This museum, located in downtown Nanaimo, provides an in-depth look at the city's history, from its Indigenous roots to its growth as a coal mining town.

Coal Mining History: One of the museum's most notable displays is dedicated to Nanaimo's coal mining past. Visitors can go through a mock mine, replete with mining tools and artifacts, and learn about the lives of miners and their families.

Indigenous Heritage: The museum's Indigenous gallery focuses on the Snuneymuxw First Nation's culture and history. Exhibits include traditional tools, art, and a detailed look at the Snuneymuxw's interaction with the land and water.

Temporary exhibits: The museum frequently holds temporary exhibits on a variety of topics, from local art to historical events, so there is always something new to see.

Comox Air Force Museum

The Comox Air Force Museum, located at CFB Comox, offers an intriguing glimpse into Canada's military aviation history. The museum is dedicated to preserving and displaying the Royal Canadian Air Force's history and impact on the local community.

Aircraft and Artefacts: The museum's collection contains a variety of aircraft, from historic planes to modern jets, as well as uniforms, medals, and other military memorabilia. The outdoor Heritage Air Park houses numerous restored aircraft, allowing visitors to get up close to these remarkable planes.

Historical Exhibits: The exhibits cover a wide range of military aviation topics, including the Air Force's role in World War II, the Cold War, and peacekeeping missions. Personal anecdotes and interactive displays contribute to the vividness of these historical events.

Library and Archives: The museum's library and archives are invaluable resources for historians and aviation enthusiasts, containing a variety of documents, photographs, and data about Canada's air force history.

Quw'utsun Cultural and Conference Centre in Duncan

This cultural center in Duncan provides an immersive journey of the Cowichan people's customs and heritage, who are part of the Coast Salish Nations.

Traditional Arts and Crafts: Visitors can see craftsmen at work making traditional Cowichan sweaters, sculptures, and other items. The center's gift shop sells real Indigenous art and handmade products.

Cultural Performances: The center includes regular performances of traditional music, dance, and storytelling, which are a fascinating way to learn about Cowichan culture and history.

Educational Programs: Guided tours and educational programs provide a fuller understanding of the Cowichan people's way of life, their relationship to the land, and their attempts to preserve and promote their traditional legacy.

U'mista Cultural Centre in Alert Bay

The U'mista traditional Centre is dedicated to preserving and presenting the Kwakwaka'wakw people's traditional legacy. This center, located in Alert Bay, serves as a light for cultural education and preservation.

Potlatch Collection: The U'mista Cultural Centre's main attraction is its collection of potlatch regalia, which includes masks, headdresses, and other ceremonial objects. These artifacts were repatriated after being confiscated during the potlatch ban, giving the collection historical and cultural value.

Exhibits and displays: The center's exhibits focus on several aspects of Kwakwaka'wakw culture, such as traditional governance, art, and daily living.

Interactive displays and multimedia presentations improve the tourist experience.

Cultural Programs: U'mista offers educational programs, workshops, and cultural performances that give visitors a thorough understanding of Kwakwaka'wakw traditions and modern living.

Victoria's Chinatown, including Fan Tan Alley

Victoria's Chinatown is Canada's oldest National Historic Site, preserving the rich history and culture of Chinese immigration in British Columbia.

Historic Walking Tours: Guided walking tours of Chinatown provide light on the lives of early Chinese immigrants, their contributions to the city, and the difficulties they encountered. The Chinese Public School, the Tam Kung Temple, and the elaborate Gate of Harmonious Interest are all significant landmarks.

Fan Tan Alley: Fan Tan Alley, Canada's tiniest street, is a must-see on any visit to Chinatown. It was once home to gambling dens and opium factories, but now it houses one-of-a-kind businesses and galleries. The alley's historical importance and distinct character make it a must-see.

Chinese Canadian Museum: The Chinese Canadian Museum, which is set to open in the heart of Chinatown, will highlight Chinese Canadian history and contributions. Exhibits will cover a wide range of issues, from early immigration and settlement to contemporary accomplishments and cultural legacy.

Fort Rodd Hill and Fisgard Lighthouse National Historic Site

These nearby sites near Victoria provide an intriguing peek into the region's military and marine history.

Fort Rodd Hill: This coastal artillery fort was built in the late 1800s to protect Victoria and the Esquimalt Naval Base. Visitors can visit the well-preserved gun batteries, subterranean magazines, and barracks, learning about the lives of the soldiers stationed there.

Fisgard Lighthouse: The Fisgard Lighthouse, constructed in 1860, is the oldest lighthouse on Canada's west coast. The lighthouse keeper's residence has been converted into a museum, including displays on the lighthouse's history, marine navigation, and local shipwrecks.

Interactive Programs: Both locations provide interactive programs and guided tours, which include living historical demonstrations, children's activities, and educational workshops. These programs bring history to life and provide a better understanding of the sites' importance.

The Gulf of Georgia Cannery National Historic Site

The Gulf of Georgia Cannery, located in the historic fishing community of Steveston, provides a detailed history of Canada's west coast fishing sector.

Cannery Tour: The guided tour of the cannery takes guests through the many steps of fish processing, from unloading to canning and packing. The tour focuses on technological advancements as well as the hard work of fishermen and cannery workers.

Exhibits: The exhibits address the fishing industry's social and economic impact on the region, the many populations participating, and the current environmental challenges. Interactive displays and multimedia presentations improve the educational experience.

Educational Programs: The cannery provides educational programs for schools and organizations, which include hands-on activities and workshops. These programs are intended to involve people of all ages and provide a better awareness of the fishing industry's history and contemporary concerns.

BC Forest Discovery Centre, Duncan

The BC Timber Discovery Centre is a 100-acre open-air museum dedicated to the history and effects of British Columbia's timber sector.

Historical Exhibits: The exhibits feature logging equipment, historic steam locomotives, and a rebuilt logging camp. Visitors can learn about the growth of logging techniques and the lives of the workers who helped shape the industry.

Train Rides: The center has a narrow-gauge railway that provides train rides through the woodland surroundings. The beautiful journey offers a unique view of the center's displays and the surrounding area.

Educational Programs: Schools and groups can participate in educational programs and workshops that focus on sustainable forestry methods, conservation, and the history of the forest industry. Interactive activities and guided tours enrich the educational experience.

Craigdarroch Castle, Victoria.

Craigdarroch Castle is a spectacular Victorian-era house that reflects the affluent lifestyle of the late nineteenth century.

Guided tours: Guided tours of the castle lead tourists through its magnificently restored rooms, which feature antique furnishings, fine woodwork, and stained glass windows. The visits shed light on the history of the Dunsmuir family, who built the castle, as well as the social dynamics of the time.

Historical Exhibits: Exhibits span a wide range of Victorian life, including fashion, home life, and technological breakthroughs of the time. The castle's large collection of artifacts and archival papers provides a complete history of the period.

Educational Programs: The castle provides educational programs for schools and organizations, which include hands-on activities and themed tours. These programs aim to engage participants and create a greater understanding of Victorian history and culture.

Vancouver Island's museums and historical sites provide a rich tapestry of experiences that bring the past to life. These institutions offer a thorough glimpse at the island's unique history, from Indigenous origins and early European settlement to industrial progress and Victorian splendor.

Visitors to these locations can obtain a better understanding of the people and events that shaped Vancouver Island, leading to greater respect for its cultural and historical richness. Whether you're a history buff, an art fan, or just inquisitive about the past, Vancouver Island's museums and historical sites offer an entertaining and educational trip through time.

Beaches and Coastal Wonders on Vancouver Island

Vancouver Island, located on Canada's west coast, is known for its beautiful beaches and coastal sceneries. From rough cliffs pummelling by Pacific seas to tranquil sandy stretches ideal for a family picnic, the island provides a wide range of coastal experiences.

Exploring these coastal beauties not only connects you with nature but also provides insight into the region's ecological diversity and historical significance. This book delves into the most noteworthy beaches and coastal attractions on Vancouver Island, outlining what makes each one special and worth visiting.

Long Beach: A Surfers' Paradise.

Long Beach, located in the Pacific Rim National Park Reserve, is possibly Vancouver Island's most famous beach. It stretches across 16 kilometers and gives a beautiful view of sand, surf, and sky.

Surfing and Water Sports: Long Beach is a surfers' paradise, attracting visitors from all over the world. Its regular waves and various breaks appeal to both new and seasoned surfers. Numerous local surf schools, including Pacific Surf School and Surf Sister, provide lessons and equipment rentals.

Beachcombing and Wildlife Watching: The extensive shoreline of Long Beach is ideal for beachcombing. Visitors can discover unusual shells, driftwood, and the occasional piece of sea glass. The beach is also a great place to see wildlife, including bald eagles, sea otters, and migratory grey whales.

Scenic walks and Photography: Long Beach is a photographer's dream, with its broad views and spectacular coastline scenery. Walking along the beach, particularly after sunset, provides numerous opportunities for spectacular photographs. The Pacific Ocean and surrounding jungle add to the beach's natural splendor.

Chesterman Beach: Family-Friendly Fun.

Chesterman Beach, in Tofino, is a popular destination for both locals and visitors. Its mild waves and sandy shoreline make it perfect for families and casual beachgoers.

Tide Pools & Marine Life: At low tide, Chesterman Beach shows a variety of tide pools rich with marine life. These natural aquariums can be explored by both children and adults, and they contain starfish, crabs, and anemones. It is a hands-on approach to learning about the local ecosystem.

Beach Activities & Rentals: The beach is ideal for a range of activities such as paddleboarding, kayaking, and beach volleyball. Several local stores provide rentals and lessons for people who want to try their hand at these activities.

Frank Island and Sunset: Frank Island is located near the southern end of Chesterman Beach and is accessible by foot during low tides. The island offers a unique vantage point for breathtaking sunset views.

The evening sun spreads a golden tint across the beach, making for an ideal finale to a day of exploration.

Rathtrevor Beach - A Natural Playground

Rathtrevor Beach Provincial Park, in Parksville, is famed for its long, sandy beach and shallow, mild water. It's an excellent place for families and wildlife enthusiasts.

Camping and picnicking: The park has great camping amenities, with sites set among thick trees and only a short walk from the beach. Picnic spaces are ideal for family meals, as they include tables and fire pits.

Birdwatching and Nature Trails: Rathtrevor Beach is a bird viewers' paradise, especially during the spring migration, when thousands of birds stop to eat on the exposed tidal flats. The park also has various nature trails that wind through the coastal forest and along the seashore, allowing visitors to witness a variety of species.

Sandcastle Building and Beach Games: The broad sandy beach is ideal for constructing sandcastles and playing beach games. At low tide, the shallow waters spread far out, providing children with a huge playground to explore.

Mystic Beach: A Hidden Gem.

Mystic Beach, located on the Juan de Fuca Trail, is a hidden gem that provides a more remote and rough coastal experience.

Hiking & Access: Mystic Beach is accessible only via a walk along the Juan de Fuca Trail. The trailhead is at China Beach, and the journey to Mystic Beach is around 2 kilometers. The walk winds through thick rainforests crosses suspension bridges, and provides views of the shore.

Waterfall and Natural Beauty: One of Mystic Shore's features is the waterfall that drops immediately onto the shore. This unusual feature, combined with the sea caves and rock formations, makes it an ideal location for photography and exploration.

Camping and Seclusion: Mystic Beach allows camping for those looking for a more adventurous experience. Because of the beach's remote location and restricted accessibility, visitors can frequently enjoy it in relative seclusion, accompanied by the sounds of the water and the forest.

Sombrio Beach: Adventurer's Delight.

Sombrio Beach, another hidden treasure along the Juan de Fuca Trail, is a favorite spot for surfers, hikers, and adventurers.

Surf and bodyboarding: Sombrio Beach is noted for its superb surfing conditions, which draw surfers from all over the island. The beach's rough shoreline and strong currents make it ideal for skilled surfers.

Hidden Waterfall: A short walk from the main beach area leads to a secluded waterfall nestled in a steep canyon. This peaceful area is ideal for taking a refreshing dip or simply relaxing under the falling water.

Wilderness Camping: Sombrio Beach, like Mystic Beach, offers backcountry camping for individuals who want to immerse themselves in nature. The beach's remote position and steep topography offer a true wilderness experience, including hiking, wildlife watching, and stargazing.

Botanical Beach: Ecological Wonder.

Botanical Beach, located in Juan de Fuca Provincial Park in Port Renfrew, is well-known for its abundant tide pools and unique marine life.

Tide Pools & Marine Biology: Botanical Beach is a treasure trove for marine biologists and environment lovers. The tide pools are home to a variety of marine species, including sea stars, sea urchins, and anemones. The beach's unique geological characteristics provide an ideal home for these critters.

Educational Opportunities: Interpretive signs and guided tours give educational information about the ecology of tidal pools and the larger marine environment. Visitors may learn about the intertidal zone and the adaptations that let marine life flourish in this unpredictable environment.

Scenic Trails and Views: The Botanical Beach Loop Trail provides breathtaking views of the coast and adjacent greenery. The trail is well-marked and appropriate for all ages, giving it an excellent opportunity to explore the area and appreciate its natural beauty.

Parksville Beach: Family-Friendly Fun.

Parksville Beach, located in the heart of Parksville, is a popular destination for families and beachgoers seeking a combination of relaxation and recreation.

Parksville Beach Festival: Every summer, Parksville Beach celebrates the Parksville Beach Festival, which includes the world-famous sand sculpture competition. Talented artists from all over the world construct breathtaking sand sculptures, transforming the beach into an open-air gallery.

Swimming and Water Activities: The beach's mild, shallow waves are ideal for swimming and wading. The calm waves make it a perfect location for young children and anyone looking for a leisurely swim in the ocean.

Playground and Amenities: Parksville Beach has good amenities, such as playgrounds, picnic spaces, and restrooms. Tennis courts, volleyball nets, and a skateboard park may all be found at the nearby Parksville Community Park.

San Josef Bay: Remote Beauty

San Josef Bay, located in Cape Scott Provincial Park, provides a lonely and pristine coastline experience for those prepared to go off the usual road.

Hiking & Access: San Josef Bay is accessible via a 2.5-kilometer hike from the trailhead at the end of the San Josef Bay Road. The walk is quite easy, making it accessible to the majority of visitors.

scenic beauty and seclusion: San Josef Bay is renowned for its breathtaking beauty, which includes sea stacks, sandy beaches, and lush woodlands. The secluded setting provides a sense of privacy and tranquility, making it ideal for those seeking a calm retreat.

Camping and Exploration: Camping is permitted in San Josef Bay, allowing visitors to fully experience the area's natural splendor. Visitors can explore the beach, climb local trails, and enjoy the peacefulness of this natural coastal area.

Vancouver Island's beaches and coastal beauties provide an astonishing variety of experiences, from the boisterous surf culture of Long Beach to the peaceful, hidden gems of Mystic Beach and San Josef Bay. Each coastal locale has its distinct beauty, offering chances for adventure, relaxation, and connection with nature. Whether you're surfing the waves, exploring tidal pools, hiking through lush forests, or simply taking in the breathtaking ocean vistas, the island's beaches will leave you with amazing memories and a profound appreciation for nature. As you visit these coastal beauties, you'll see the diverse beauty and ecological complexity that make Vancouver Island a true haven for beachgoers and outdoor enthusiasts.

Events & Festivals on Vancouver Island

Vancouver Island is a bustling location that holds a variety of events and festivals all year. These festivals highlight the island's unique culture, rich heritage, and vibrant arts sector. From seasonal festivals and musical extravaganzas to sporting events and competitions, Vancouver Island has something for everyone. This guide takes a detailed look at the most prominent events and festivals, allowing you to organize your vacation around these exciting occasions.

Seasonal Festivals and Events.

Seasonal festivities in Vancouver Island commemorate the changing seasons and the riches that they bring. These activities celebrate local traditions, agricultural heritage, and the island's natural beauty.

Spring: Cherry Blossom Festival.

The Cherry Blossom Festival in Victoria welcomes spring with a breathtaking display of cherry blossoms that transform the city streets into a sea of pink and white.

Blossom Viewing: Take a stroll through Beacon Hill Park, Government House Gardens, and other attractive areas to admire the flowers. Many sections are lined with cherry trees, which provide a beautiful backdrop for photos and leisurely walks.

Cultural Activities: The festival frequently incorporates Japanese cultural events including tea ceremonies, calligraphy workshops, and traditional music performances, which represent Victoria's historical ties with Japan.

Summer: BC Seafood Festival.

The BC Seafood Festival, held in the Comox Valley, celebrates the island's unique maritime tradition and abundance of fresh seafood.

Seafood Tastings: Enjoy a range of seafood delicacies produced by local chefs, such as salmon, oysters, clams, and more. The festival has a large number of food kiosks, each with a distinct twist on local seafood.

Cooking Demonstrations: Watch renowned chefs demonstrate their culinary skills and provide advice for making seafood meals. The demonstrations are both educational and entertaining.

Family Activities: The festival offers activities for all ages, including touch tanks, educational exhibits, and cookery courses for children, making it a family-friendly event.

Fall: Cowichan Valley Wine Festival.

The Cowichan Valley Wine Festival, held each autumn, honors the region's thriving winemaking industry. It's an excellent opportunity to visit the local vineyards and sample the greatest wines Vancouver Island has to offer.

Winery Tours: Participating wineries offer guided tours that provide insight into the winemaking process. Learn about the various grape varietals farmed in the region, as well as the distinct qualities of Cowichan Valley wines.

Wine Tastings: Sample award-winning wines like Pinot Noir, Chardonnay, and others. Many vineyards include meal pairings, which enhance the tasting experience.

Special activities: The festival frequently includes special activities such as vineyard dinners, live music performances, and wine seminars, providing a well-rounded experience for wine lovers.

Winter: Festival of Trees.

Victoria's Festival of Trees: is a popular holiday event that brings the community together to celebrate the season while also raising funds for a good cause.

Businesses and organizations decorate Christmas trees, which are then displayed at the Bay Centre and various sites throughout the city. Each tree is distinctively themed and elegantly decorated, resulting in a spectacular holiday environment.

Fundraising Activities: The festival is a fundraiser for the BC Children's Hospital Foundation, with a variety of activities and events geared to benefit pediatric care and research.

Holiday Performances: Local choirs, musicians, and dance groups will perform as part of the festival's entertainment roster. These acts enhance the festive atmosphere and provide family-friendly entertainment.

Music and Art Festivals

The numerous music and arts festivals on Vancouver Island highlight the island's strong art sector. These events showcase local talent while attracting performers and artists from all around the world.

Victoria Symphony Splash

Victoria Symphony Splash is one of North America's largest annual outdoor symphonic events, attracting tens of thousands of attendees to Victoria's Inner Harbour.

Symphony Performance: The event's highlight is a full orchestral concert on a floating stage in the inner harbor. The concert includes a combination of classical and modern pieces, concluding with a stunning fireworks show.

Family Zone: The event features a Family Zone with games and entertainment for youngsters, making it a fun and welcoming environment for families.

Food and Beverage: Enjoy a choice of food and beverage options from local vendors while listening to music and seeing the beautiful waterfront views.

Tofino Jazz Festival

The Tofino Jazz Festival celebrates jazz music in one of the most picturesque venues on Vancouver Island.

The event together local and international performers for a weekend of spectacular performances.

performances: Attend performances at numerous venues in Tofino, ranging from intimate café settings to bigger outdoor stages. The roster features a variety of jazz styles, from traditional to current.

seminars: Attend seminars and masterclasses given by professional musicians. These seminars are available to all skill levels and offer an unparalleled opportunity to learn from the greatest.

Community Events: The festival frequently incorporates community events such as jam sessions, art exhibits, and film screenings, which add to the cultural diversity of the event.

Salt Springs National Art Prize

The Salt Spring National Art Prize (SSNAP) is a notable biennial event highlighting modern

Canadian art. The prize, which is held on Salt Spring Island, recognizes and supports artistic talent.

Art display: The event includes a display of the finalists' work, which was chosen from hundreds of submissions from throughout Canada. The exhibition features a diverse range of mediums, including painting, sculpture, photography, and mixed media.

The awards gala is a highlight of the event, where the winners are revealed and prizes are presented. It's a celebratory event for artists, collectors, and art fans alike.

Artist Talks and Workshops: Throughout the event, attendees can attend artist talks and workshops that provide insights into the creative process and the contemporary art scene in Canada.

Sports Events and Competitions

The various landscapes of Vancouver Island make an ideal setting for a wide range of sporting events and competitions. The island hosts a variety of events for both athletes and spectators, including marathons, cycle races, sailing regattas, and surfing contests.

The Victoria Marathon

The Victoria Marathon is one of Canada's greatest running events, attracting athletes from all around the world. The marathon offers spectacular views of Victoria's waterfront and historical monuments.

Race Options: The event offers a full marathon, half marathon, 8K road race, and a kids' run for runners of all ages and abilities. The beautiful route takes runners through the center of Victoria, passing notable landmarks including the Parliament Buildings and Beacon Hill Park.

Training Clinics: Participants can prepare for the event by attending training clinics and group runs. These clinics offer useful information on training, nutrition, and injury prevention.

Finish Line Celebrations: The finish line area is alive with activity, featuring live music, food sellers, and an awards presentation. It's a joyous atmosphere that recognizes the accomplishments of all attendees.

RBC GranFondo Whistler

The RBC GranFondo Whistler: is a prominent cycling race that takes cyclists on a magnificent route from Vancouver to Whistler, with a stop on Vancouver Island along the way.

Cyclists can pick from several demanding routes, ranging from the 122 km GranFondo to the more difficult 152 km Forte. Each route has beautiful views of the Pacific coast, lush woods, and mountainous terrain.

Support and Logistics: The event provides complete support, including aid stations, medical help, and mechanical support, to ensure that all riders have a safe and fun ride.

After crossing the finish line in Whistler, bikers can enjoy a post-ride celebration featuring food, beverages, live entertainment, and the opportunity to discuss their experiences with other cyclists.

Tofino Rip Curl Pro

The Tofino Rip Curl Pro is Canada's largest and longest-running surf competition, held each year in the surf mecca of Tofino.

Surfing Competitions: The event includes competitions in three categories: men's, women's, and juniors. Surfers from around Canada and abroad vie for the coveted championships and awards.

Beach Activities: The event offers a range of beach activities, including surfboard demos, yoga sessions, and beach cleanups, making it a fun and engaging experience for spectators.

Live Music & Entertainment: In addition to surfing, the event features live music performances, food trucks, and vendor booths, resulting in a bustling festival atmosphere on the beach.

Swiftsure International Yacht Race

The Swiftsure International Yacht Race is the greatest sailing event in the Pacific Northwest, bringing sailors from all over the world to Victoria's Inner Harbour.

Racing Classes: The event includes several racing classes, including the long-distance Swiftsure Lightship Classic, the Cape Flattery Race, and the Juan de Fuca Race. Each event presents unique difficulties and rewards, putting players' abilities and stamina to the test.

Spectator Activities: Spectators can watch the race from several viewing spots along the shoreline. The Inner Harbour is a bustling hub of activity, featuring food vendors, live music, and displays from marine-related businesses and organizations.

Post-Race Celebrations: Following the race, there are several post-race celebrations for both sailors and spectators, including award ceremonies, parties, and social events.

Vancouver Island's events and festivals provide a diverse range of experiences that highlight the island's culture, natural beauty, and community spirit. Whether you prefer seasonal festivals, music, and arts, or sporting competitions, there is something for everyone. These events not only entertain and inspire but also promote a sense of community and belonging among both locals and visitors. Exploring Vancouver Island's bustling events and festivals will reveal the destination's distinct charm and energy.

Practical Information for Travelers to Vancouver Island

Vancouver Island is a place that offers breathtaking scenery, a rich culture, and a variety of activities. To make your journey as joyful and stress-free as possible, come prepared with practical information on safety, health services, finances, and staying connected. This extensive handbook delves into these critical areas of travel on Vancouver Island.

Safety & Security

Ensuring your safety and security when traveling is critical. Vancouver Island is generally a safe area to visit, but as with any other vacation, it's crucial to keep informed and exercise caution.

General Safety Tips.

Personal Safety: Vancouver Island is known for its welcoming communities and low crime rates. However, it is always advisable to be vigilant of your surroundings, particularly in urban places at night.

Avoid remote regions and, whenever feasible, travel in groups.

Emergency Services: Dial 911 for police, fire, and medical assistance. Emergency services on Vancouver Island are dependable and effective.

Natural Hazards: Be mindful of natural hazards such as wildlife interactions, particularly when hiking or camping. Bears and cougars roam the island's wilderness sections. Always store food securely, make noise while trekking, and adhere to local wildlife safety guidelines.

Road Safety

Driving Conditions: The roads on Vancouver Island are well-maintained, however conditions might change. Snow and ice may fall in some regions throughout the winter, especially at higher elevations. Make sure your car has appropriate tires and that you are prepared for shifting weather conditions.

Speed Limits and Restrictions: Follow the posted speed limits and traffic restrictions. Speed limits in urban areas are typically 50 km/h, whereas highway speeds range from 80 to 110 km/h. Seat belts are required, and using a cell phone while driving is strictly prohibited unless hands-free.

Wildlife on Roads: Drive with caution, especially at dawn and twilight, when wildlife is more active. Deer, elk, and other animals commonly cross highways, so keep an eye out and drive slowly in wildlife-rich regions.

Water Safety

Swimming and Water Activities: The island provides several chances for swimming, kayaking, and other aquatic activities. Always adhere to local guidelines and cautions. Many beaches have chilly water all year, so be aware of hypothermia.

Boating and fishing: Make sure your vessel has the proper safety equipment, such as life jackets and communication systems. Check the weather forecast before going out, and notify someone of your plans.

Health and Medical Services

Access to health and medical services is an important concern for all travelers. Vancouver Island has a variety of healthcare facilities to meet different needs.

Hospital and Clinics

Major hospitals on the island include the Royal Jubilee Hospital and Victoria General Hospital in Victoria, the Nanaimo Regional General Hospital in Nanaimo, and the Comox Valley Hospital in Courtenay. These hospitals provide complete medical services, including emergency care.

Walk-In Clinics: Non-emergency medical needs can be addressed in walk-in clinics in most towns and cities. These clinics can treat minor injuries, diseases, and basic healthcare needs without an appointment.

Emergency Medical Services

Emergency Numbers: In the event of a medical emergency, dial 911. Emergency medical services (EMS) are available throughout the island, ensuring fast response and transportation to medical facilities.

First Aid: Carry a basic first aid kit, especially if you plan on doing any outdoor activities. Familiarise yourself with basic first aid practices and the whereabouts of nearby medical institutions.

Pharmacies and Medicines

Pharmacies are frequently present in cities and small towns. Major chains include Shoppers Drug Mart, London Drugs, and Rexall. Pharmacists can offer information on over-the-counter drugs and fill prescriptions.

Travel Health Insurance: Make sure you have enough travel health insurance to cover medical emergencies, including evacuation if needed. Check your policy information before leaving, and bring your insurance card with you.

Money & Currency Exchange

A successful vacation experience requires efficient financial management. Understanding the local currency and currency conversion choices can allow you to stay prepared.

Currency: The Canadian Dollar (CAD) is the official currency of both Vancouver Island and Canada. Banknotes are available in denominations of $5, $10, $20, $50, and $100, and coins in denominations of 5 cents (nickel), 10 cents (dime), 25 cents (quarter), $1 (loonie), and $2 (toonie).

Credit and debit cards: are commonly accepted around the island, including at restaurants, shops, and hotels. The most often accepted cards are Visa and MasterCard. American Express and Discover are accepted at select locations.

Currency Exchange

Major banks, including RBC, TD Canada Trust, Scotiabank, and CIBC, provide currency exchange services. Credit unions such as Coast Capital Savings and Island Savings also offer these services.

Dedicated currency exchange offices can be found in major locations like Victoria and Nanaimo. They frequently offer competitive conversion rates and a wide range of foreign currencies.

ATMs: Automated Teller Machines (ATMs) are widely available and provide a quick option to withdraw Canadian dollars with a debit or credit card. Be mindful of any overseas transaction fees that your bank may levy.

Tips and Taxes

Tipping: Tipping is traditional in Canada. In restaurants, a tip of 15-20% of the total bill before taxes is customary. Taxi drivers, hairdressers, and hotel staff should be tipped 10-15%. It is also traditional to tip tour guides and service personnel.

British Columbia levies a 7% Provincial Sales Tax (PST) and a 5% federal Goods and Services Tax (GST) on the majority of its goods and services.

Some things, including groceries, are exempt from PST.

Connectivity and Communication

Staying connected while traveling is critical for safety, convenience, and communication with loved ones. Vancouver Island offers a variety of networking and communication alternatives.

Mobile Phones and SIM Cards

Mobile Coverage: Rogers, Bell, Telus, and their subsidiaries (Fido, Virgin Mobile, Koodo) are Canada's major mobile network providers. These carriers provide extensive coverage across Vancouver Island, while some outlying locations may have restricted service.

SIM Cards: If you're visiting from another country, consider getting a local SIM card for your unlocked phone. SIM cards are sold at cell carrier stores, electronics retailers, and some convenience stores. Prepaid plans often include data, talk, and text choices.

Internet Access

Free Wi-Fi: is readily available in hotels, cafes, restaurants, and public libraries. Many tourist destinations and rail hubs have complimentary Wi-Fi connectivity.

Portable Wi-Fi Devices: If you need reliable internet access while traveling, consider renting a portable Wi-Fi device. These devices may link several devices to the internet and are accessible through a variety of rental businesses.

Communication Apps

Messaging and calling: Use messaging apps like WhatsApp, Facebook Messenger, and iMessage to communicate with family and friends. These apps are useful for texting, making audio and video conversations, and sharing photographs and videos.

Download important travel apps such as navigation, language translation, and local information. Apps such as Google Maps, TripAdvisor, and Yelp can improve your travel experience by giving instructions, reviews, and recommendations.

Postal Services

Canada Post runs multiple post offices on Vancouver Island, offering mail and parcel delivery services. Post offices can be found in cities, rural areas, and some retail locations.

To mail postcards or letters, stamps can be purchased at post offices, convenience stores, and some souvenir shops. Drop your mail in any Canada Post mailbox or post office.

Additional Practical Tips

Weather and Clothing

Climate: Vancouver Island's climate is warm and temperate, with distinct seasons. Summers are warm and dry, while winters are damp and mild. Coastal locations receive more rainfall, although the interior might be cooler in winter.

Packing Tips: Bring clothing appropriate for the season and activities you intend to conduct. Layers are advised for adjusting to shifting temperatures. Remember to pack waterproof clothing and sturdy footwear, especially if you plan to explore the outdoors.

Language & Communication

Official Language: English is the major language spoken on Vancouver Island. French is the second official language of Canada, however, it is not widely spoken in this region.

Communication Etiquette: Canadians are recognized for being courteous. Use kind language, such as "please" and "thank you," and respect personal space. When addressing locals, it is customary to use their titles and last names unless they request to be addressed by first name.

Electricity and Adapters

Electrical Standards: Canada has a 120V, 60Hz electrical system with Type A and Type B plug sockets. If your gadgets operate on a different voltage or plug type, you will want a voltage converter and/or plug adaptor.

Chargers and equipment: Make sure your electronic equipment is compliant with the local voltage. Many new chargers and electronics are dual voltage, but you should always verify before traveling.

Vancouver Island provides a diverse range of experiences for visitors, from natural beauty and cultural richness to outdoor adventures and urban attractions. Understanding practical knowledge regarding safety, health services, finances, and connectivity will help you have a seamless and pleasurable vacation. Whether you're trekking through the island's pristine forests, discovering its lovely towns, or indulging in its gastronomic delights, being well-prepared will allow you to make the most of your trip to this enchanting place.

Conclusion

Vancouver Island captivates travellers' hearts with its diverse scenery, rich cultural past, and limitless options for adventure. Whether you enjoy the outdoors, history, food, or relaxation, the island has something for everyone. As you prepare for your journey, here are some final thoughts and suggestions to make your trip as fun and memorable as possible.

Tips for an unforgettable visit

While having an itinerary is vital, allowing for spontaneity can result in some of the most memorable encounters. Vancouver Island is full with hidden jewels and unexpected joys, so make time in your itinerary to explore and discover at your leisure.

Research and Reservations: Make reservations for popular activities and lodging well in advance, especially during peak seasons. This ensures that you reserve your spot and avoid last-minute disappointments.

Stay Informed: Monitor local news and weather forecasts. Weather conditions can vary quickly, particularly in coastal and mountainous regions. Staying informed allows you to plan your activities correctly.

Pack wisely: Packing adequately for the island's diverse climate and activities is critical for a relaxing vacation. Here are some important factors to consider:

Layered Clothing: The weather might change dramatically throughout the day. Layered clothing allows you to respond to changing conditions, keeping you comfortable while trekking, sightseeing, or eating out.

Outdoor clothing: If you intend to go hiking, kayaking, or beachcombing, pack appropriate clothing such as strong boots, a waterproof jacket, and sunscreen.

Include a basic first-aid kit, any medications, and personal hygiene goods. It is also advisable to bring reusable water bottles to stay hydrated while reducing plastic waste.

Respect nature and local culture: The beauty of Vancouver Island is preserved because to the respect and care shown by its tourists and people. You can help to ensure the long-term viability of this gorgeous location by adhering to local guidelines and engaging in responsible tourism.

Leave No Trace: When exploring natural places, adhere to the Leave No Trace philosophy. Dispose of rubbish correctly, stick to authorised pathways, and respect wildlife and their habitats.

Support local businesses by shopping: dining, and using their services. This not only improves your experience, but it also benefits the island's economy and community.

Learn about and respect Indigenous cultures: Vancouver Island is home to many varied Indigenous communities with rich cultural heritages. Learn about their history and traditions, and respect their land and customs.

Stay connected and safe: While enjoying your vacation, make sure to stay connected and prioritise your safety.

Emergency Contacts: Make a list of emergency contacts, including local emergency services, your lodging, and family or friends. This is especially critical if you're travelling to distant places.

Connectivity: Mobile coverage is generally adequate, but some outlying regions may have limited service. Consider hiring a portable Wi-Fi device if you need consistent internet access throughout your trip.

Capture the moments: Your journey to Vancouver Island will be full with breathtaking sights and experiences. Documenting these occasions will allow you to appreciate your memories long after you return home.

Photography: Bring a camera or make sure your smartphone is ready to take high-quality images.

Vancouver Island has several photo options, ranging from breathtaking landscapes to lively fauna.

Journaling: Keep a trip journal to capture your ideas and impressions. This personal touch enriches your recollections and might make an excellent keepsake.

Final words

Vancouver Island combines the spirit of adventure, the tranquilly of nature, and the warmth of community. As you embark on your tour, allow the island's particular appeal to inspire you.

Enjoy the moments: Whether you're standing on a craggy cliff overlooking the Pacific, eating a meal crafted with locally sourced ingredients, or hearing the history of the island's Indigenous peoples, savour every minute. The pace of life on Vancouver Island promotes reflection and appreciation.

Connect with the locals: The people of Vancouver Island are noted for being friendly and welcoming. Engaging with locals can enhance your experience by providing insight into the island's culture, hidden beauties, and best-kept secrets. Ask for recommendations or start a conversation.

Embrace the Unexpected: Travel often shocks us, and Vancouver Island is no exception. Accept the unexpected, whether it is a sudden change in weather, an unforeseen diversion, or a fortuitous encounter with wildlife. These experiences frequently become the highlights of your journey.

Reflect on your journey: As your stay on Vancouver Island comes to an end, pause to reflect on your adventure. Consider what you've learned, the beauty you've seen, and the relationships you've formed. Travel can transform, and your experiences on the island will leave an indelible impression.

Vancouver Island offers breathtaking natural beauty, a rich cultural legacy, and numerous options for adventure and relaxation. By planning ahead of time, packing wisely, respecting the environment and local traditions, and embracing the island's spirit, you may create a vacation experience that is not only enjoyable but also deeply meaningful.

As you leave, you'll have recollections of towering woods, exquisite beaches, dynamic villages, and, perhaps most importantly, a sense of belonging to a place that encourages exploration and reflection. Vancouver Island is more than just a tourist destination; it is an experience that will linger with you long after you leave. Enjoy your journey, and may it be full of surprises, joy, and inspiration.

Appendix

Useful Apps

Google Maps: For navigation and finding local attractions.

TripAdvisor: For reviews, recommendations, and travel planning.

Yelp: For finding restaurants, cafes, and other businesses.

Airbnb: For unique lodging options.

Booking.com: For hotel reservations.

Expedia: For booking flights, hotels, and car rentals.

WhatsApp: For messaging and calls.

Facebook Messenger: For staying in touch with friends and family.

Skype: For international calls.

BC Ferries: For ferry schedules and booking.

WeatherCAN: For up-to-date weather forecasts.

Vancouver Island News: For local news and updates.

Emergency Contacts

Emergency Services (Police, Fire, Ambulance): 911

Royal Jubilee Hospital (Victoria): +1 250-370-8000

Nanaimo Regional General Hospital: +1 250-754-2141

Comox Valley Hospital: +1 250-331-5900

BC Poison Control Center: +1 800-567-8911

Tourist Information: +1 250-385-5711 (Victoria Visitor Centre)

FAQs

What is the best time to visit Vancouver Island?

- The best time to visit is from May to September when the weather is warm and outdoor activities are in full swing. However, each season offers unique experiences, such as whale watching in spring and fall.

Do I need a car to get around Vancouver Island?

- While having a car provides flexibility, especially for exploring remote areas, it's possible to get around using public transport, ferries, and tour services. Major towns and cities have good transit systems.

Are there any health risks on Vancouver Island?

- Vancouver Island is generally very safe, with high-quality healthcare facilities. Standard travel health precautions apply, such as staying hydrated, using sunscreen, and being aware of wildlife safety guidelines.

What should I pack for a trip to Vancouver Island?

- Pack layered clothing for variable weather, waterproof gear, sturdy walking shoes, and outdoor activity essentials. Don't forget sun protection and any personal medical supplies.

Can I use US dollars on Vancouver Island?

- While Canadian dollars are the official currency, some places may accept US dollars, though the exchange rate may not be favorable. It's best to use Canadian currency or credit/debit cards.

Travel Checklist

Essentials:

- Passport or ID
- Travel insurance documents
- Credit/debit cards and some cash (Canadian dollars)
- Travel itinerary and reservations

Clothing:

- Layered clothing (sweaters, jackets)
- Waterproof jacket and pants
- Comfortable walking shoes and hiking boots
- Swimsuit (if planning to swim)
- Hat and sunglasses

Personal Items:

- Medications and first aid kit
- Toiletries
- Reusable water bottle
- Sunscreen and insect repellent

Technology:

- Smartphone and charger
- Portable power bank
- Camera (optional)
- Plug adapter (if coming from outside North America)

Outdoor Gear:

- Backpack for day trips
- Binoculars (for wildlife viewing)
- Travel guidebook or maps

Travel Itineraries

3-Day Travel Itinerary

Day 1: Victoria

Morning: Explore the Inner Harbour, visit the Royal BC Museum.

Afternoon: Lunch at Fisherman's Wharf, stroll through Beacon Hill Park.

Evening: Dinner at a downtown restaurant, enjoy live music or theater.

Day 2: Saanich Peninsula

Morning: Visit Butchart Gardens.

Afternoon: Tour local wineries, lunch at a vineyard.

Evening: Return to Victoria, explore Chinatown and Bastion Square.

Day 3: Gulf Islands

Morning: Ferry to Salt Spring Island, visit Ganges Village.

Afternoon: Explore local markets and artisans.

Evening: Return to Victoria, farewell dinner.

5-Day Travel Itinerary

Day 1-2: Victoria and Saanich Peninsula

Follow the 3-day itinerary for the first two days.

Day 3: Cowichan Valley

Morning: Drive to Cowichan Valley, visit Duncan's Totem Poles.

Afternoon: Wine tasting and lunch at a local vineyard.

Evening: Explore downtown Duncan or stay at a countryside B&B.

Day 4: Nanaimo and Parksville

Morning: Drive to Nanaimo, explore the Harbourfront Walkway.

Afternoon: Visit Newcastle Island, lunch at a waterfront café.

Evening: Drive to Parksville, walk along Rathtrevor Beach.

Day 5: Comox Valley

Morning: Drive to Comox Valley, visit Comox Air Force Museum.

Afternoon: Explore Courtenay and Cumberland, visit local shops and galleries.

Evening: Dinner in Courtenay, stay overnight.

7-Day Travel Itinerary

Day 1-5: Follow the 5-day itinerary.

Day 6: Tofino and Ucluelet

Morning: Drive to Tofino, explore Long Beach.

Afternoon: Visit Tofino Botanical Gardens, lunch in town.

Evening: Sunset at Chesterman Beach, dinner at a local seafood restaurant.

Day 7: Pacific Rim National Park and Return

Morning: Hike the Rainforest Trail or visit Hot Springs Cove.

Afternoon: Explore Ucluelet, visit the Wild Pacific Trail.

Evening: Return to Nanaimo or Victoria for departure.

Made in the USA
Monee, IL
26 January 2025